MW00573771

REGGAE, RASTAFARI, AND
THE RHETORIC OF SOCIAL CONTROL

REGGAE, RASTAFARI, AND THE RHETORIC OF SOCIAL CONTROL

By Stephen A. King

With contributions by
Barry T. Bays III and P. Renée Foster

University Press of Mississippi / *Jackson*

This volume is supported in part by Delta State University.

An earlier version of chapter five appeared in *Popular Music and Society* 22.3 (1998) : 39–60. An earlier version of chapter six appeared as "The Co-Optation of a Revolution: Rastafari, Reggae, and the Rhetoric of Social Control" in *Howard Journal of Communications* 10: 77–95; copyright 1999 by *Howard Journal of Communications* and reproduced by permission of Taylor & Francis, Inc., http://www.routledge-ny.com. An earlier version of the epilogue appeared in *Marketing in the Century Ahead: Proceedings of the Sixteenth Annual Atlantic Marketing Association Conference*, 11–14 October 2000. Ed. Jerry W. Wilson, 2000: 85–94.

www.upress.state.ms.us

Copyright © 2002 by University Press of Mississippi
All rights reserved
Manufactured in the United States of America

10 09 08 07 06 05 04 03 02   4 3 2 1

Library of Congress Cataloging-in-Publication Data
King, Stephen A., 1964–
    Reggae, Rastafari, and the rhetoric of social control / by Stephen A. King ; with contributions by Barry T. Bays III and P. Renée Foster.
    p.   cm.
Includes bibliographical references (p.) and index.
ISBN 1–57806–489–9 (cloth : alk. paper)
    1. Reggae music—Jamaica—History and criticism. 2. Music—Jamaica—Social aspects. 3. Rastafari movement—Jamaica—History. I. Bays, Barry T. II. Foster, P. Renée.

ML3532 .K55 2002
781.646'097292—dc21   2002001734
                    British Library Cataloging-in-Publication Data available

to J. Michael Hogan

To My RASTA Soul Bro,
Enjoy The Read....
Irie,
Stylu

CONTENTS

Contents

ACKNOWLEDGMENTS

The foundation of this book is the dissertation I completed at Indiana University in 1997. I first would like to acknowledge the contributions of my dissertation chair, J. Michael Hogan. Recognized as one of the leading dissertation advisors in the field of speech communication, Mike Hogan played a pivotal role in organizing the overall plan of the dissertation and suggesting countless ways to improve the scope, style, substance, and direction of the dissertation. This book is dedicated to him. I would also like to extend my appreciation to the other members of the dissertation committee: Carolyn Calloway-Thomas, Dennis Conway, and John L. Lucaites.

The book's collaborators played a key role in transforming the dissertation into a book. Barry Bays, an instructor of music at Delta State University (DSU), assisted with the "musical instrumentation" sections in chapters 1–3. P. Renée Foster, assistant professor of marketing at DSU, helped me revise the epilogue. In addition, she spent countless hours reading and editing numerous drafts of the dissertation and the book manuscript.

A special word of thanks is reserved for my editor, Craig Gill, whose enthusiasm, patience, and editorial direction helped me complete the project. I would also like to express my gratitude to the anonymous reviewer of

Acknowledgments

an earlier draft of the manuscript. Without a doubt, his/her comments and suggestions helped improve the quality of the book.

There are several individuals and organizations that played an invaluable role during my successful trip to Jamaica. Indiana University awarded me a Student-in-Aid Grant for Dissertation Research that helped subsidize my trip to Jamaica. While in Jamaica, the library staff at the University of the West Indies (UWI), the African-Caribbean Institute of Jamaica, and the National Library of Jamaica assisted in the gathering of important primary and secondary documents on the Rastafarian movement and reggae music. I thank Don Robotham, UWI University Dean, for granting me the position of research scholar at the university. A special word of thanks goes to Carolyn Cooper, Barry Chevannes, Dermot Hussey, and Rex Nettleford, who were so generous to take time out of their busy schedules to be interviewed for this project.

I extend my thanks to the faculty in the Division of Languages and Literature at DSU for their support and encouragement during the completion of this project. In addition, the DSU Interlibrary Loan Department was instrumental in locating and securing important primary and secondary documents necessary to complete this book.

I also need to recognize friends who contributed to this project in some way or another. To name just a few: Holly Baxter, Julie Boyd, Dan Butler, Becky Carrier, Selina Carver, Jim Cherney, Darryl Clark, Jeff Danon, Mark Felton, John Galuska, Dexter Gordon, Dick Jensen, Tom Jewell, the Hopkins brothers, Stephanie Houston-Grey, Ilon Lauer, Nancy McGahey, Clayton Millard, Randy Osborn, Ben Parker, Dan and Kelly Schowalter, Jan Schuetz, Kevin Shaw, Tessa Simpson, Helen Tate, Julie Thompson, Neill Vaughan, Thom Vaughn, Miss Kitty, and Lewis.

Finally, I express my admiration, gratitude, and love to my parents. Thanks for making this all possible.

INTRODUCTION

Rastafarianism is the first mass movement among West Indians preoccupied with the task of looking into themselves and asking the fundamental
question, *Who Am I?* or *What Am I?*

—Dennis Forsythe

From the shantytowns of Kingston, Jamaica, to the cobblestone streets of
Great Britain, reggae music has been a powerful and liberating voice for the
poor and oppressed. In the last thirty years, reggae stars Bob Marley, Burning
Spear, and Alpha Blondy have sung "redemption" songs—messages of
human rights and universal love—in a "Babylonian" world of civil unrest,
political instability, and economic collapse. Bob Marley and the Wailers'
1979 single, "Zimbabwe," was a national anthem for the Pan-African freedom fighters during the Rhodesian civil war (Fergusson 56). Marley's influence was so great that Zimbabwe's national flag is now based on Rastafarian colors which, in turn, are based on Ethiopia's flag (Kerridge 343).
According to Kevin O'Brien Chang and Wayne Chen, authors of the
acclaimed *Reggae Routes: The Story of Jamaican Music*, reggae music served
as protest music during Nicaragua's civil war, China's Tienanmen Square

demonstrations, and the fall of the Berlin Wall (3). Jay S. Kaufman elaborated on reggae's international popularity and political influence: "The world-wide acceptance of Reggae . . . provides evidence that the power of music to influence political and social change is not limited to Jamaican society, but is something more fundamental and universal" (9).

In its native Jamaica, reggae concerts also have provided a meeting ground for warring political factions. In two notable cases, Bob Marley headlined the 1976 Smile Concert and the 1978 One Love Peace Concert in Jamaica; both concerts attempted to unite Jamaica's two political parties, the People's National Party (PNP) and the Jamaica Labour Party (JLP). At the One Love Peace Concert, Marley invited the leader of the PNP, Michael Manley, and his avowed enemy, JLP leader Edward Seaga, on stage for a symbolic handshake of peace. As Marley would say of his music: "[Reggae music] is like the news. The music influence the people, the music do everything fe [for] the people. The music tell the people *what* to do, in Jamaica" (Davis, "Bob Marley" 91).

Reggae's influence and popularity both within and outside Jamaica reflects its "third-world" origins. In particular, reggae's roots are embedded in the historical conditions of Jamaican slavery and colonialism. Since the arrival of Columbus in 1494, Jamaica has been a pivotal point of European exploitation of the indigenous population (Arawak Indians), African slaves, and land resources for profit and prestige. Jamaica's early history was "one long tale of sad intrigue, human suffering, lawlessness, and immoral profit, at the center of which were the African slaves—the ancestors of present-day Jamaicans" (Barrett 29).

Since Jamaica's independence in 1962 from Great Britain, many black Jamaicans have lived with chronic unemployment, street violence, and inadequate housing. While Jamaica's affluent society attends school and works at middle- to upper-class jobs, a majority of young poor black Jamaicans live in "oil drums and out in the open with maybe a jagged scrap of corrugated iron propped by a few splintering sticks" (Davis, *Bob Marley* 42).

The Jamaican masses use music to counteract oppression and degradation. In fact, music is one of the few avenues for the Jamaican poor both to create a distinctly black Jamaican identity and to vent "years of pent-up suffering, dehumanization and frustration under the white man's hegemony" (Hylton 26). Jamaican popular music has undergone musical and lyrical changes, becoming increasingly political and revolutionary in tone. By the late 1970s, reggae embodied this musical evolution, viewed by many as "the very expression of the historical experience of the Jamaican working class, unemployed and peasants" (L. Johnson, "Reggae Rebellion" 589). Lyrically, reggae musicians protest against food shortages, inadequate housing, crime, police brutality, illiteracy, political violence, homelessness, and oppression.

In another important way, reggae music's association with the Rastafarian movement has awakened an African consciousness in many black Jamaicans. Erna Brodber, a native Jamaican who has written extensively on reggae music, has described reggae as providing a new orientation to Africa:

> We were glad to hear this new sound. It relaxed us. We took off our make-up, we washed our hair and left it natural; we took off our jackets and ties and made ourselves comfortable in shirt jacks. And we understood at a personal level that for us black Jamaicans, there were two orientations: a mulatto-orientation and an Afro-orientation, the latter having been submerged in our consciousness. The persistent reggae beat—and the lyrics it carried—was partly responsible for awakening this consciousness. (Brodber, "Black Consciousness" 54)

For more than thirty years, Bob Marley and the Wailers have exemplified reggae's role as a protest music. In many of his songs, Marley attacked the destructive nature of poverty by focusing on hunger ("No Woman No Cry" [*Natty Dread*]), urban crime ("Concrete Jungle" [*Catch a Fire*]), political violence ("Rat Race" [*Rastaman Vibration*]), police brutality ("I Shot the Sheriff" [*Burnin'*]), and slavery ("Slave Driver" [*Catch a Fire*]).

Despite the fact that Marley and other reggae artists have become popular throughout the world, the Jamaican government on occasion has forbidden Jamaica radio stations from airing various forms of Jamaica's popular music. In 1964, the ska song "Carry Go Bring Come" was banned from Jamaican radio for criticizing JLP prime minister Alexander Bustamante (Kaufman 9). During the 1972 national political campaign, the JLP banned several "anti-JLP" reggae songs, including the Wailers' "Small Axe" (Waters 102). With the exception of Reggae Sunsplash, reggae concerts, by the early 1980s, were banned in Jamaica supposedly because "of the violence associated with some concerts and dances" (Winders 67). In the view of some political officials, according to historian James A. Winders, reggae songs called attention "to certain features of Jamaican life" that the government, "anxious to attract tourist dollars," preferred to hide (71).

Paradoxically, the Jamaican government often has used reggae music to promote its own social and political ends. First, Jamaican politicians, on numerous occasions, have integrated reggae music into their political campaigns. In the 1972, 1976, and 1980 elections, Michael Manley hired reggae musicians to play at political rallies. In Jamaican society, according to musician Jay S. Kaufman, reggae music has dominated "the political arena to such an extent that elections were almost won or lost by the popularity of their campaign songs" (9).

In recent years, the Jamaican government also has promoted reggae music and the exotic Rastafarian culture as the "'official' culture of the island" (Cosgrove 46). In the late 1970s, the Jamaican government promoted reggae music to attract tourists to revive a dying economy. In 1982, the Jamaica Tourist Board (JTB), with the help of white American promoter Barry Fey, assembled a vacation concert package that drew over forty-six thousand visitors to Jamaica (George and Fergusson 62). Even Jamaica's most popular reggae festivals, Reggae Sunsplash and Reggae Sumfest, are supported by the government because the events help support Jamaica's tourist industry.

Since the 1990s, Rastafarian images and reggae have become increasingly important in promoting Jamaica's tourist industry. The Jamaican government and its supporters market the Rastafarian movement and reggae music as part of Jamaica's "cultural heritage." In a wide range of promotional materials, travel brochures highlight reggae's "happy" and "peaceful" themes, while obscuring the music's lyrics of social rage. In much the same way, Rastafarians are portrayed as eager and happy participants, willing to help fulfill a tourist's "fantasy vacation." Yet, this depiction largely ignores the movement's historical record of confronting and resisting colonialism, poverty, and institutional racism.

THE ORIGINS AND EARLY HISTORY
OF THE RASTAFARIAN MOVEMENT

The Rastafarian movement between 1870 and 1958 evolved in three distinct stages: (1) Marcus Garvey and Ethiopianism (1870–1930); (2) the coronation of Haile Selassie as emperor of Ethiopia and the formation of early Rastafarian churches (1930–1949); and (3) the emergence of the Youth Black Faith as a militant faction within the Rastafarian movement (1949–1958).

The origins of the Rastafarian movement can be traced, in part, to Jamaican black nationalist Marcus Moziah Garvey. Born in Jamaica on August 17, 1887, Garvey left school at the age of fourteen to work as a printer's apprentice. In 1910, Garvey left Jamaica and traveled extensively throughout Central and South America, becoming involved in radical journalism. In 1912, Garvey left for England and, over the next two years, became interested in African culture and history. Convinced that blacks must unify to overcome their oppression, Garvey returned to Jamaica in 1914 and established the Universal Negro Improvement Association (UNIA)(Waters 37). Two years later, Garvey traveled to the United States and established UNIA offices in Harlem, New York. The UNIA produced the international weekly paper, the *Negro World*, and organized a chain of black-owned small businesses, from grocery stores to laundromats to factories manufacturing black dolls (Berry and Blassingame 409–10). By 1920, Garvey boasted of a UNIA membership of two million blacks.

Garvey was responsible for influencing the Rastafarian movement's theme of repatriation to Africa. Garvey originated the slogan, "Africa for Africans," and he sponsored the Black Star Steamship Line, a shipping corporation founded to transport blacks to Africa. According to anthropologist Barry Chevannes, Garvey "linked the dignity and equality of blacks to their ability to claim a land they could call their own, one in which they could be their own master" (*Rastafari* 95).

Garvey also inspired the Rastafarian's belief in a living black God. Garvey was influenced by a "particular brand of black nationalism" called "Ethiopianism" (Campbell, *Rasta* 49). Originating in South Africa during the 1870s, Ethiopianism was a secessionist church movement rebelling against missionary churches that condoned the practice of white colonial rule and apartheid (Campbell, *Rasta* 47–50). Challenging the prevailing argument that blacks were judged inferior in the Bible, Ethiopianism articulated a new, more positive role for blacks in the Bible. Influenced by Ethiopianism, Garvey "gloried in the African past and taught that God and Christ were black" (Berry and Blassingame 410).

Garvey's success was short-lived. In 1925, he was sentenced to serve a five-year sentence in an Atlanta penitentiary for mail fraud. In 1927, U.S. President Calvin Coolidge commuted Garvey's sentence, and he was then deported to Jamaica. For the next ten years, Garvey attempted unsuccessfully to revive the UNIA. Although ridiculed by Jamaica's dominant society, Garvey was venerated by Jamaica's lower classes as a "saint" and worshiped by the Rastafarian movement as a "prophet." Scholars of the Rastafarian movement have pointed to two distinct events that influenced Rastafarians to perceive Garvey as the movement's prophet. According to political scientist Horace Campbell, many of Garvey's followers believed that the UNIA slogan, "'Princes come out of Egypt, Ethiopia shall stretch forth her hands to God,'" prophesized a ruler emerging in Africa to "lead all black people to freedom" (*Rasta* 64). Chevannes pointed to Garvey's 1929 play entitled *The Coronation of the King and Queen of Africa.* The play dramatized the crowning of an African king (*Rastafari* 94–5). Within a year, Garvey's fictional play would come "true."

The official coronation of Ras Tafari Makonnen as the new emperor of Ethiopia in 1930 signaled the second phase in the development of the Rastafarian movement. During the coronation, Makonnen took the throne name, Haile Selassie I, along with other royal titles, including "'King of Kings, Lord of Lords, Conquering Lion of the Tribe of Judah, [and] Elect of God and Light of the World'" (Chevannes, *Rastafari* 42). Receiving international media exposure, color pictures of the events were published

Introduction

throughout the world, and newsreels of the ceremonies gave many blacks in the United States and the Caribbean their first glimpse of Ethiopia (Campbell, *Rasta* 70). When Jamaica's national newspaper, the *Daily Gleaner*, published photos of Selassie's coronation, some of Garvey's followers in Jamaica consulted their Bibles and subsequently believed Selassie was literally the "'King of Kings,'" the black messiah prophesized by Garvey (Chevannes, *Rastafari* 42).

Leonard Howell has been identified as the first Rastafarian preacher in Jamaica. In the winter of 1932, Howell encouraged Jamaicans to reject the authority of the King of England and to give their loyalties to the new emperor of Ethiopia (Campbell, *Rasta* 71). Howell sold pictures of Haile Selassie as future "passports" to Ethiopia. As expected, Jamaica's colonial government objected to Howell's anti-colonial rhetoric. In 1934, the police arrested Howell and his deputy, Robert Hinds, for breaking Jamaica's sedition laws. After a speedy trial, Howell was sentenced to two years—and Hinds to one year—of hard labor (Campbell, *Rasta* 71).

The Rastafarians' ability to survive during periods of heavy persecution was a testament to the movement's diversification and lack of a centralized leadership. In other words, the movement is a collection of groups who operate without a central leader. Leonard Barrett, a noted scholar on the Rastafarian movement, clarified the movement's disdain for central leadership:

> No leader has arisen to unite the separate branches of the movement and there is no desire to do so. The Rastafarians are deathly afraid of leaders because they feel that a leader would destroy the movement. There are still "leading brethren," but these are men around whom various groups are organized. Their power is mostly organizational, they do not speak for the members as leaders, but simply serve as an inspiration for their specific groups. (172)

Despite the movement's decentralized nature, there are common linkages among the various groups. Nagashima has suggested that "[m]utual understanding, respect, and love has been emphasised in order to consolidate their fellowship and faith" (25). According to Douglas R. A. Mack, in 1961 "when the Rastafarian brethren were being bombarded by the

Jamaican institutional society . . . [t]he love, unity, and communal spirit that existed among us, made us weather the storm" (68). Chevannes claimed that the Rastafarians' historical commitment to diversification stemmed from the powerful influence of Revivalism, a rural peasant religion in Jamaica (*Rastafari* 119).

While Howell and Hinds were languishing in prison, the Rastafarian movement continued to gain new followers. In addition to Howell's group, there were at least three other Rastafarian groups in existence during the 1930s. In one, Rastafarian preacher Joseph Hibbert emphasized the powers of the occult to his members (Chevannes, *Rastafari* 124–6). Another called the "King of Kings Mission" followed Hinds and sponsored baptism and fasting (Chevannes, *Rastafari* 124–44). A third group, under the leadership of Archibald Dunkley, rejected the Revival practice of spirit possession, or the belief that good or evil spirits could invade and temporarily take control of a human body (Chevannes, *Rastafari* 126).

While each exemplified a different style of worship and emphasized distinctive aspects of the Rastafarian "doctrine," there were at least four overarching themes uniting these factions. First, all four leaders condemned Jamaica's colonial society. Second, all believed repatriation to Africa was the key to overcoming oppression. Third, all these early preachers advocated nonviolence. Finally, all four groups worshiped the divinity of Haile Selassie.

In 1940, four years after his release from prison, Howell formed a Rastafarian community called Pinnacle. Pinnacle was an old estate in the hills of St. Catherine, one of Jamaica's fourteen parishes. According to one observer, Howell

> was revered in the Rastafarian community and his word was "law" in Pinnacle. A council of elders was established to assist in the daily administration of the camp, and to maintain discipline among the brethren who dwelt there. . . . Brother Howell often rode his horse around the community from time to time in order to inspect the crops and camp activities. Brethren would run, following his horse, anywhere he went. The community became prosperous and Brother Howell became very "well off." (Mack 60–1)

Boasting a membership of over sixteen hundred Rastafarians, Pinnacle became a self-sufficient "farming" community (Campbell, *Rasta* 94). Since Howell's cash crop was marijuana, the Pinnacle community "gave to the Rastafari[an] movement its close association in the mind of the public with ganja" (Chevannes, *Rastafari* 122). The cultivation of ganja and the rumors of violence in the area drew police suspicions. In 1941, the police raided Pinnacle and arrested twenty-eight Rastafarians on charges of cultivating a dangerous drug. Once again, Howell was standing in court pleading his innocence. The Rastafarian leader was sentenced to serve another two years in prison (Campbell, *Rasta* 95).

While early Rastafarian leaders preached political withdrawal and non-violence, a group of young radicals emerged from the poorer sections of West Kingston in 1949 to form a more "militant" Rastafarian group called the Youth Black Faith. According to Chevannes, while early Rastafarian leaders "encountered police harassment," these new radicals were on "fire with the doctrine," and often provoked confrontations with authorities (*Rastafari* 154, 159). Despite the Youth Black Faith's "militant" tactics, the Rastafarian movement remained a largely apolitical movement until the mid- to late 1960s.

In the 1950s, the Youth Black Faith initiated the tradition of wearing dreadlocks in the Rastafarian movement. According to Campbell, Rastafarians grow dreadlocks by "washing the hair and allowing it to dry without combing, brushing or treating it in any way" (*Rasta* 96). Although the Rastafarians pointed to the Bible to justify the dreadlock hairstyle, the move was controversial because in Jamaica unkempt hair was associated with "mad dialects" and "outcasts" (Chevannes, *Rastafari* 158). The decision to wear dreadlocks caused such a fierce debate within the Youth Black Faith that the movement split into two factions. In a 1994 interview, Chevannes argued that the "House of Dreadlocks" sponsored this new "dangerous" trend, while the "House of Combsomes" maintained the necessity of combing one's hair. It was not until the late 1960s that the dreadlock tradition became universally acceptable within the movement.

The Youth Black Faith also was responsible for creating the movement's unique language. Although English is the official language of Jamaica, many Jamaicans speak patois (pronounced "pa-twa"). Patois combines Standard English and African languages. The Rastafarians experimented with patois and created their own distinctive language. Chevannes discussed the use of the most important aspect of Rastafarian talk, the personal pronoun, "I."

> To the Rastafari this is the same as the Roman numeral *I*, which follows the name "Selassie." "I" substitutes for "me" and for "mine." The religious meaning behind this substitution is that the Rastafari is also part of God, and if God is a visible, living man, it must mean that the Rastafari is another Selassie, another "I." Because everyone is an "I," one does not say "we" for plurality, but says "I and I." As the most central word in the Rastafari speech, "I" transforms other words as well. "Brethren" pronounced in the dialect as "bredrin," becomes "Idrin"; "eternal," "Iternal"; "hour," "Iowa"; "times," "Iimes"; "creator," "Ireator"; and so forth. (*Rastafari* 167)

The term "downpressor" was also unique to the Rastafarian movement. Rastafarians substituted "downpression" for "oppression." The Rastafarians believed that language shaped human perceptions, and they altered words to fit their philosophy (Sanders 62). For example, Rastafarians maintained that the sound of the word "oppression" projected the image of one uplifting the oppressed out of poverty. The term "downpression" clearly indicated that the oppressor was keeping the oppressed down—trapped in the ghettos and slums of Jamaica. In a similar way, the Rastafarians changed the word "understand" to "overstand." The Rastafarians believed they do not have to "go under" to gain knowledge and wisdom.

The Youth Black Faith's aggressive stance symbolized the escalating tension between Rastafarians and Jamaican authorities during the 1950s. For example, in 1954, Jamaica's security forces succeeded in dismantling Howell's Pinnacle community. During the raid, police arrested an estimated 163 Rastafarians on numerous charges including the cultivation of a dangerous drug (Barrett 87). In 1960, Howell was placed in an asylum for the mentally ill. A year earlier, a Rastafarian and a police officer clashed at Coronation Market located in West Kingston. During the incident, local vendors sided with the Rastafarian, thus encouraging police retaliation (Ferguson 62). Shortly after this altercation, police raided Back-O-Wall, a Rastafarian shantytown in West Kingston, and forcibly shaved Rastafarians' dreadlocks (Semaj, "Inside Rasta" 8). Bongo Israel's own mistreatment at the hands of the police supports the movement's claim of police brutality: "We had to watch out for the police, come in and destroy us. They catch us on the street. They cut our locks" (*Stepping Razor*).

As police intimidation of the Rastafarians increased, repatriation emerged as the movement's most urgent demand. In 1955, a representative from the Ethiopian World Federation (EWF) announced that Selassie was building a Merchant Navy with the hope of eventually providing transport to Ethiopia for Jamaicans (Barrett 90). Founded by Haile Selassie's cousin in 1937, the EWF's purpose was to unite several groups who were supporting Ethiopia during its war with Italy (Campbell, *Rasta* 76). According to Leonard Barrett, the announcement of Selassie's "repatriation" plan "created what might literally be called a religious revival among the Rastafarians." The Rastafarian movement, according to Barrett, "doubled its membership almost overnight" (90).

While the Rastafarian movement would prove unsuccessful in achieving the dream of repatriation, the movement had become by the late 1950s an irritating thorn in the side of the Jamaican government. Meanwhile, musical experiments involving Rastafarian musicians, such as drummer "Count" Ossie, and musicians associated with a popular form of music known as "ska" began to forge a four-decade relationship between the Rastafarian movement and Jamaica's popular music. As a result, the popular music of Jamaica became more than a mode of entertainment; it became perhaps the chief medium of political and social commentary and, ultimately, a threat to the government. This study explores how that politicization of Jamaican popular music came about and how, ultimately, the government co-opted the politics of reggae.

PUBLIC AND SCHOLARLY INTERPRETATIONS OF THE RASTAFARIAN MOVEMENT

Since the Rastafarian movement's inception in the 1930s, the response has ranged from "curiosity" to open "hostility" (Forsythe, "West Indian" 63). Not surprisingly, the *Daily Gleaner*'s early press coverage of the movement reflected the latter response; stories exaggerated the movement's ability to undermine Jamaica's theme of "national unity," and criticized members of the movement as "dope fiends," "malcontents," and "violent revolutionaries." In much the same way, the pioneering work of anthropologist George E. Simpson in the 1950s was fraught with inconsistencies, inaccuracies, and a lack of sensitivity to cultural differences common to some ethnographic studies of the period. Even as late as 1982, Ivor Morrish in his book, *Obeah, Christ and Rastaman: Jamaica and Its Religions*, criticized the movement for "its total ignorance of the world, economic affairs, and any sense of history" (89).

Unfortunately, the work of Morrish and others increasingly reflected a decidedly anti-Rastafarian bias rather than a clear understanding of the movement's religious/spiritual philosophy, political goals, and contributions to Jamaica's cultural heritage. Indeed, the recent work of several noted Rastafarian and reggae scholars has rehabilitated the Rastafarians' image in Jamaica and dispelled a number of the myths surrounding the movement's religious and/or political philosophy.[1]

Yet, the existing research has not considered a number of important issues. First, several studies on reggae music are bound by a one-dimensional focus on song lyrics. For example, several widely recognized and well-respected books on reggae music do not include an in-depth analysis of the music itself.[2] In addition, many of these sources fail to use specific categories to examine the protest themes of Jamaica's popular music. Thus, this study pursues a series of questions about the persuasive functions of protest lyrics derived from Smith, Stewart, and Denton's typology of social movement rhetoric. By comparing, for example, the protest themes of ska to early reggae, it is argued that the "hero" figure in Jamaica's popular music became increasingly more aggressive and political in nature. Moreover, it is important to appreciate the relationship between Jamaica's popular music and its influence on the development of the Rastafarian movement. For example, in chapter 5, it is argued that while international reggae music popularized the movement, it also created a number of divisions within the Rastafarian movement and attracted a number of pseudo-Rastafarian groups to the movement. As a result, the Rastafarian movement seemingly became more of a "cultural fad" to some observers rather than a serious religious or political movement. Further, this study considers how the counter-pressures exerted by the Jamaican government and its surrogates also contributed to the evolution of the music. For example, efforts to censor ska, an early form of reggae music, resulted in the creation of a "cleaner," and less offensive, form of that music.

Second, researchers need to examine systematically the Jamaican establishment's strategies of social control. Over the years, scholars have studied the rhetoric of social control or how establishments attempt to avert protests by social movements. While some scholars suggested that Jamaica's security forces implemented physical force to arrest and imprison members of the movement, most studies neglected to analyze all of the strategies used by the Jamaican authorities to control the movement. More important, many of these studies failed to indicate whether these strategies were ever effective in controlling the movement.3

Third, scholars have not discussed how the Jamaican establishment co-opted the Rastafarian movement for their own purposes, most notably for the promotion of Jamaica's growing tourism industry. In the epilogue, it is argued that Rastafarian images and reggae music were co-opted into a symbol of Jamaica's cultural heritage and transformed into a tourist attraction.

This study will comprehensively trace how Jamaica's protest music has changed both lyrically and musically over a twenty-one-year period, and how the Jamaican government has attempted to silence or co-opt these voices of protest. Part 1 examines the relationship between agitation and control in Jamaica from 1959 to 1971. Chapter 1 focuses on the origins of reggae, examining its roots in the form of popular music known as ska (1959–1965). During this era, the fast, cheerful sounds of ska reflected the optimism of Jamaica's independence from colonial rule. While ska did hint at Rastafarian themes, the music expressed more "personal" than "political" protest. Chapter 2 explores the short-lived but influential protest music known as rocksteady (1966–1967). This chapter will consider the role of the "Rude Boys," a youth rebellion in Jamaica, in the development of a more aggressive, political music. A tension between violence and peace distinguished rocksteady as a transitional form between ska and early reggae. Chapter 3 discusses the emergence of early reggae music (1968–1971), noting how the Black Power movement in Jamaica played a significant role in coalescing Jamaica's dissident groups. In particular, the once apolitical Rastafarian movement became increasingly politicized, as evidenced in the more aggressively political themes of early reggae songs. Chapter 4 investigates the Jamaican government's response to the growing politicization of the Rastafarian movement during this entire period, from 1959 to 1971. The government and its surrogates used a variety of control strategies, from evasion to more aggressive strategies of coercion and suppression.

Part 2 investigates the tension between agitation and control from 1972 to 1980. Chapter 5 reveals how the Rastafarian movement and reggae music became an international phenomenon after 1972. During this period, U.S. record companies successfully marketed a "new" and "improved" reggae music to international audiences. While promoting reggae as a new brand of revolutionary music, record companies such as Island Records ironically modified reggae's sound in order to appeal to white audiences. Chapter 6 examines how the government under the leadership of Prime Minister Michael Manley employed an entirely new strategy for responding to the challenge of Rastafarians as reggae grew in popularity. Rather than suppress the music, Manley co-opted it, hiring reggae musicians to play at political rallies and integrating Rastafarian themes into his political rhetoric.

Introduction

The epilogue examines how the Jamaican government and the Jamaica Tourist Board (JTB) used reggae music and Rastafarian images to promote the movement and the music as part of Jamaica's cultural heritage. The conclusion of the study will elaborate on the contributions of this research to the study of social movements, the rhetoric of social control, and protest music.

Part One
(1959–1971)

Chapter One

SKA AND THE ROOTS OF RASTAFARIAN MUSICAL PROTEST

To the casual listener, "ska" may appear to be nothing more than some form of speedy and spirited reggae. This is not entirely inaccurate. Ska is actually the pop-based precursor to reggae.

—Dale Turner

By the late 1950s, a newfound optimism permeated Jamaica's warm trop-ical breezes. In a country with a history of slavery, institutionalized racism, class disparity, and economic dependence, this optimism appeared justified, at least at first glance. Despite its troubled past, Jamaica over the next few years would gain its national independence and experience an economic boom lasting until the late 1960s. The leaders of one of Jamaica's leading political parties, the Jamaica Labour Party (JLP), were excited by the prospect of independence. Yet they also realized the island was experienc-ing a host of sociopolitical problems, from overcrowding to crime. While the government launched a vigorous national campaign to stress Jamaica's transition to independence as a positive, uplifting event, "[n]epotism, violence and political victimisation came to characterise the transition from colonialism to neo-colonialism" (Campbell, "Rastafari" 10).

These political tensions coincided with the emergence of a new musical form known as ska. Ska was a mixture of mento, a Jamaican indigenous musical form, American jazz, and rhythm and blues.[1] On the surface, ska was a happy, content—even cheery—music. But if one listened closely between the polyrhythmic pulses of the music, ska was as deceptive as the government's attempt to paint the country with a color-blind palette of national unity. Ska may have sounded happy, but it also expressed a musical angst rooted in the tenement houses and yards of West Kingston, a dilapidated area of open sewers, rampant unemployment, and rival political gangs.

Despite the fact some ska songs were routinely banned from Jamaican radio stations, popular critics and music scholars generally have failed to appreciate their protest message. Erna Brodber, an observer of Jamaican music, has contended that Jamaican ska was not a medium of protest, claiming that most of the songs spoke of "morals and with love" and were little more than "re-issues of folk songs" ("Black Consciousness" 59). Writing in *The Black Scholar*, Patrick Hylton agreed that early ska songs were primarily love songs (27). In the same vein, other scholars have claimed that the music's lyrics "tended to be light, [and] were generally about love and love-making" (Alleyne 118), concluding that ska closely resembled a Caribbean music known as calypso (Winders 68). Jamaican native and longtime observer of Jamaican music, Pamela O'Gorman, has dismissed ska as little more than a "regional variant of a broad U.S. style, namely rhythm and blues" (86).

As Jamaica's leading popular music historian, Garth White, has observed, however, "critical social commentary and protest were in ska almost from its inception" ("Mento" 39). Although few observers have acknowledged ska's protest themes, ska actually represented the first form of a popular protest music, albeit a "mild" protest against social and political conditions in Jamaica. Ska songs suggested more a politics of passive suffering rather than active resistance. Yet, ska played a significant role in creating a musical "community" of both Rastafarians and those sympathetic to the movement, and it gave early expression to the Rastafarian's social and political ideology. Lyrically, ska promoted Rastafarian ideology through faint themes of repatriation and the introduction of the term "Mount Zion," the Rastafarian's heaven in Africa. Instrumentally, the ska song "Oh Carolina" featured Rastafarian drumming, and even the instrumental songs bore titles such as "Another Moses" and "Babylon Gone," highlighting the movement's belief in the divinity of Ethiopian emperor Haile Selassie and the hope for deliverance from oppression, or "Babylon." With the advent of ska, Rastafarians thus began to explore a new mode of political expression, popular music, with far more reach than their traditional outlets: street preaching, church sermons, pamphlets, and word of mouth within Rastafarian communes.[2] In the end, ska portended the development of popular music as the chief communicative medium of the Rastafarian movement.

JAMAICA: FROM COLONIALISM TO INDEPENDENCE

Following the arrival of Columbus in 1494, Jamaica became one of many Caribbean countries to be colonialized by European powers. From 1494 to 1655, the Spanish nearly extinguished Jamaica's indigenous population, the Arawak Indians, while plundering the island for silver and gold. When the English became Jamaica's new colonial rulers in 1655, they brought another source of forced labor, the West African slave. By the end of the seventeenth century, African slaves were being brought to Jamaica in increasing numbers to cultivate the vast fields of sugar cane. Even after the end of slavery in 1834, Jamaica continued to be under the thumb of British colonial rule, supporting a small white planter class and a large peasantry consisting mostly of former slaves. The white planter class denied the peasants' independence by restricting the sale of land. Since most of the peasants could not obtain land, they were forced to work for the white planter class, subject to deplorable working conditions and cheap wages, as low as a penny a day (Beckford and Witter 40–1).

In 1938, a national workers' strike set in motion a series of events that led ultimately to Jamaica's independence in 1962. Rural sugar and banana workers and urban dockworkers rebelled against low wages and demanded improved working conditions. During the national strike, several were killed, hundreds were injured, and many others were jailed for their participation in the rebellion (Post 276–84).

To pacify the enraged workers, the British Crown established a Royal Commission, led by Lord Moyne, to investigate the workers' demands (Beckford and Witter 62). The Moyne Commission established several new policies, including steps to establish representative self-government in Jamaica. Meanwhile, Jamaica's colonial office conceded to the leaders who voiced the workers' grievances against the colonial state, Alexander Bustamante and Norman Washington Manley (Beckford and Witter 61). In 1938, Manley became the leader of Jamaica's first mass political party, the People's National Party (PNP), and Bustamante assumed the leadership of one of Jamaica's first organized labor unions, the Bustamante Industrial Trade Union (BITU).

In 1942, Manley and Bustamante disagreed over the PNP's political role in Jamaica. Manley envisioned the PNP's mission as seeking Jamaica's constitutional independence, while Bustamante's interests were to "secure the new relationship of direct bargaining of the laboring class with the ruling class" (A. Brown, *Color, Class, and Politics* 103). Tension between the two leaders became so great that Bustamante left the PNP and used his BITU to launch Jamaica's second political party, the Jamaica Labour Party in 1943.

Following the split, the relationship between the two parties remained tense; the conflict often moved from simmering hostility to open warfare. The PNP was considered "left wing," sponsoring economic and social reform, a high profile in international affairs and, at times, a socialist government. The JLP, in contrast, was described as a "right-wing" party maintaining a conservative ideology that favored capitalism, free enterprise, and a close link with western countries.[3] A number of rival political parties, including the People's Political Party (PPP), never achieved much success in Jamaica. Led by Barrister Millard Johnson, the PPP was a socialist party that ran political advertisements in Jamaica's national newspaper, the *Daily Gleaner*, advocating the redistribution of wealth, eradication of racial discrimination, and developing economic and social ties to Africa (B. Johnson 25).

From 1944 to 1962, Jamaica's political leaders and the British Crown worked on a plan for Jamaica's full independence. In 1944, the British Crown signed into law a new Constitution, granting Jamaica Universal Adult Suffrage (Beckford and Witter 62). Ultimate authority for Jamaica's internal and external affairs still rested with the governor-general who represented the British monarchy in Jamaica. By 1957, however, Britain began to undertake serious steps to relinquish control of Jamaica because of the financial burden the Caribbean colony placed on British taxpayers (Panton 26). In 1957, the PNP implemented a Cabinet government that enabled the Jamaican government to play a more influential role in determining the nation's economic policies (Panton 26). Two years later, the PNP established Jamaica's first fully autonomous government (Panton 26). This new arrangement allowed the prime minister to assume full responsibility for all internal affairs and reduced England's authority in Jamaica to issues of foreign policy. On August 6, 1962, Jamaica finally secured full constitutional independence and became an independent parliamentary state within the British commonwealth. While the governor-general still remained officially head of the state, his role was now reduced to appearing at ceremonial events. The prime minister and his Cabinet government now had full executive power to make policy decisions in domestic and international affairs.

Less than four months before Jamaica became a sovereign nation, Manley and the PNP were voted out of office, and the JLP's Alexander Bustamante became prime minister. Bustamante presided over a remarkable economic resurgence which occurred prior to and following independence. From 1950 to 1968, Jamaica's gross domestic product (GDP), adjusted for inflation, increased 6.7 percent (Kuper 17). In 1960, the unemployment figure dipped to 13.5 percent, one of the lowest unemployment rates on record (Boyd 8–9). In addition, between 1956 and 1967, Jamaica's manufacturing sector expanded as Jamaican entrepreneurs profited from an assortment of exports, including furniture, garments, and footwear (Stone, "Power, Policy and Politics" 27). Jamaica also continued to be one of the world's leading exporters of bauxite. The Jamaican government encouraged American and Canadian companies to invest in Jamaican bauxite; bauxite continued to be

Jamaica's chief export for the next decade. As economist Derick Boyd has summarized: "The decades of the fifties and sixties were, in the main, good years for the Jamaican economy" (5).

While workers mined the "unlimited" deposits of bauxite in the hills of Jamaica, the Jamaican government also began to develop an equally appealing, less physically demanding "gold mine." In order to catch the eye of the wealthy foreign traveler, the Jamaican government actively encouraged foreign investors to expand the tourist industry on Jamaica's north coast. The sunny attractions, including Negril, Montego Bay, and Ocho Rios, sprouted new resort hotels, airport runways, and private beaches.

As foreign visitors celebrated their new tropical escape, the JLP continued to face both old and new social and political problems. There are at least four factors that plagued Jamaica as it made the transition from a British colony to an independent nation. First, Jamaica became even more economically dependent on foreign powers. The JLP and the PNP strived to emulate the "Puerto Rican Model" to create a "new" Jamaica. The effort to emulate this model, nicknamed "Operation Bootstrap," encouraged foreign investors to establish manufacturing activities in Jamaica. By 1962, Jamaica's economy was heavily tied to foreign investors, with dramatic increases in exports to Britain, the United States, Canada, and Japan. Jamaica's dependence on foreign countries turned the island into a "peripheral attachment to the international capitalist system" (Beckford and Witter 79). In the case of bauxite, for example, Jamaica possessed the raw materials but did not possess the management and technological resources. In effect, Jamaica lacked the means of processing raw materials, such as bauxite and sugar. Because Jamaica depended on foreign powers for production, the island suffered from trade deficits, high interest rates, and high fees charged for technological and management services (Beckford and Witter 79).

Second, multinational corporations continued the process of purchasing Jamaica's rural land. American and Canadian companies had taken over control of the bulk of the bauxite industry, and these multinational companies often drove small farmers from the rural areas of Jamaica's parishes,

including St. Ann and St. Elizabeth (Campbell, *Rasta* 93). Between 1943
and 1970, according to Campbell, 560,000 rural inhabitants were displaced
from Jamaica's countryside (*Rasta* 86). As these multinational corporations
purchased the farms to mine for bauxite, Jamaica's agricultural output
dropped steadily, and Jamaicans began to rely more and more on imported
food products.

Third, because of the land seizures and Britain's 1962 immigration law
that severely restricted Jamaicans from migrating to England, thousands
migrated to Kingston, Jamaica's capital city. There they suffered from unemployment, food shortages, and a high infant mortality rate. Many who could
not find work turned to hustling, prostitution, and crime. In the slums, food
shortages and disease played a significant role in a high death rate for children under four years of age. The *Life Tables for British Caribbean Countries*
indicated that, from 1959 to 1961, 5,980 out of 100,000 infant males died
during their first year of life (32). This was the highest death rate of all age
groups in Jamaica.

Fourth, with the increasing migration of the populous to the city,
Jamaica experienced a severe housing shortage. Although Jamaica's *Town
Planning Department Report* in 1961 stressed a need to redevelop some of
Kingston's poorer suburbs, including Trench Town and Kingston Pen, the
commission was unable to make any substantial changes in these areas,
building very few domiciles (3). For the very poor who could not rent a sin-
gle-story tenement or a small apartment in a government housing project,
squatting on government land became a matter of survival (Clarke 234).
As the need for housing increased and the available housing slowly turned
into crumbling tenements, middle-class Jamaicans built new houses in the
Kingston Heights. Soon, Kingston visibly displayed the contrast between
the rich and poor, as "mansions climbed up the hillsides while ghettoes
spawned along Spanish Town Road" (Beckford and Witter 74). The
increasing economic disparity between the middle and upper classes and
those crowded in the urban ghettos made Jamaica's national motto, "Out
of Many, One People," seem more and more an empty slogan.

THE RASTAFARIAN MOVEMENT: "CULT OF OUTCASTS"

During the 1950s, the Rastafarians were viewed by many in Jamaica as bearded drug addicts, a national eyesore, or a "cult of outcasts" (Patterson, "Ras Tafari" 15). The *Daily Gleaner* reported frequent clashes between Rastafarians and police, and the work of sociologist George E. Simpson confirmed the stereotype of the Rastafarians as black racists who wanted to rule over the white man (134–5). While the Rastafarian movement did indeed promote racial pride, the movement in reality posed little threat to Jamaica's ruling class. Largely lower class, politically passive, and nonviolent, most Rastafarians were committed only to repatriating members to Africa and to worshiping the divinity of Haile Selassie.[4] For the most part, Rastafarians avoided the political world, preferring meditation and prayer.

At the same time, however, the Rastafarian movement had developed a language of protest that later became prominent in Jamaica's popular music. The first of three terms important to understanding this emerging political consciousness was "Babylon," a term borrowed from the Bible but given unique meanings by the Rastafarian movement. In studying the Old Testament, the Rastafarians had "identified the Black Jamaicans as the chosen people of which the Bible spoke. In the bondage and oppression of the Hebrews in Egypt, they saw their own bondage and oppression in this latter day Babylon [Jamaica]" (Beckford and Witter 76). Since this biblical interpretation became common among Rastafarians, the term Babylon has been applied to a variety of entities that Rastafarians consider oppressive. Rastafarians have used the term Babylon to refer to the Jamaican government, the police, the Christian church, and western culture in general (Davis and Simon, "A Rasta Glossary" 69). Babylon has come to be associated with any symbol of oppression, as well as with any person who intentionally hurts others out of personal greed or prejudice (Gibson 25).

A second term that developed unique and special meanings within the Rastafarian movement was "Jah." In Rastafarian culture, "Jah" referred to former Ethiopian emperor Haile Selassie. In 1929, Jamaican black nationalist Marcus Garvey's fictional play, *The Coronation of the King and Queen of Africa,* spotlighted the crowning of an African king. In 1930, when Ras Tafari Makonnen, the great grandson of King Sahela Selassie of Shoa, was crowned emperor of Ethiopia (and renamed Haile Selassie I), many Jamaicans were convinced that he was literally the "King of Kings," the living black messiah. Many Rastafarians believed Selassie's status as a deity was a rejection of the white Christian church. The living black messiah rejected both the Bible's portrait of Jesus Christ as white and the story of his death. For the Rastafarians, "Jah" was a "symbol of resistance" to the white church (Beckford and Witter 76).

The third protest term with unique significance in the Rastafarian movement was "Mount Zion." Lamenting their own captivity in Jamaica, Rastafarians consulted their Bibles and identified their suffering with the plight of the Jews in the Bible. Consequently, Zion was torn from its biblical context and came to express the Rastafarians' hope for repatriation to Africa. Through the Rastafarian lens, Mount Zion moved from Israel to Africa. Rastafarians rejected the traditional Christian interpretation that heaven was a spiritual place "in the sky" and promoted the belief that Mount Zion was, literally, a "heaven on earth."

In the late 1950s and early 1960s, the Rastafarian movement actively began to seek repatriation to Mount Zion in Africa. In 1959, a self-declared Rastafarian "prophet," Claudius Henry, sold fifteen thousand tickets to Rastafarians and other poor Jamaicans promising repatriation back to Ethiopia on October 5 (Smith, Augier, and Nettleford 16). Many abandoned their homes, sold their belongings, and traveled long distances to the port in Kingston where Henry promised that a ship would be waiting. The tickets even included a written promise that "[n]o passport will be necessary for those returning home to Africa" (Smith, Augier, and Nettleford 16). After Henry could not deliver on his promise of repatriation, he was jailed and fined for disturbing the peace.

The arrest of Claudius Henry only served to confirm what many had already thought about the Rastafarian movement—that they were a bunch of crackpots, deluded by visions of returning to Africa. After his release from jail in December 1959, Henry became increasingly hostile toward Jamaican authorities. Preaching to the members of his Rastafarian group, the African Reformed Church, Henry's sermons often condemned the oppressive British government. During one sermon, Henry allegedly threatened the life of Prime Minister Norman Manley (Gray 50–1). On April 6, 1960, the *Daily Gleaner* announced that police, suspicious that Henry was planning to overthrow the government, had raided Henry's headquarters and found twenty-five hundred electrical detonators, plus a cache of shotguns, machetes, and dynamite ("Weapons Seized" 1). In October of that same year, Henry went to trial on a variety of charges, including treason. During his trial, Henry announced he was a "prophet" and encouraged Jamaicans to "reform themselves" and seek repatriation to Africa ("Drilled Men" 4).

In the same year, Henry's son, Ronald Henry, was training a guerrilla band of Rastafarians and sympathetic African Americans in Red Hills, a suburb overlooking Kingston. Ronald Henry and his followers had returned to Kingston from New York with the intent of overthrowing the Jamaican government (Stone, *Class, Race, and Political Behavior* 154–5). The government sent in a police force and soldiers from the Royal Hampshire Regiment, a military unit of the British command in Jamaica, and quickly suppressed the "Red Hills" incident (Barrett 98–9). The younger Henry and four of his followers were captured and sentenced to death for conspiring to overthrow the government.

In 1963, a Rastafarian "uprising" once again struck fear in the hearts of many Jamaicans. The altercation began near Montego Bay when a group of Rastafarians protested against restrictions that prohibited them from walking across the Rose Hall estate to their small plot of land. Rose Hall was quickly being transformed into a tourist attraction called Coral Gardens, and authorities feared the Rastafarian presence would frighten tourists (Campbell, *Rasta* 106). The conflict turned ugly, as a group of Rastafarians allegedly burned down a gas station, attacked a police officer with a spear, and killed eight people. The *Daily Gleaner* speculated that the Rastafarians were under the influence of drugs when they launched their "Holy Thursday rampage" ("8 Killed" 1). Within twenty-four hours, more than 150 Rastafarians were arrested on assorted charges, including vagrancy and unlawful possession of drugs and weapons ("8 Killed" 1).

Because the Rastafarian movement continuously evolved, it is difficult to describe its doctrines at any given stage of its development. At the request of some members of the Rastafarian movement, three University of the West Indies (UWI) researchers conducted two weeks of intensive research on the movement in July 1960 and summarized the movement's core beliefs in a brief pamphlet entitled the *Report on the Rastafari Movement in Kingston, Jamaica*. Their report found that the Rastafarian movement unanimously believed in the divinity of Haile Selassie and favored the repatriation of all its members to Africa. After discussions with Rastafarian members, the authors also summarized the movement's goals: to end police persecution, to improve economic conditions and access to adult education, and to strengthen human rights, including freedom of movement and speech (33–4).

Despite occasional incidents like the "Coral Gardens" uprisings, most Rastafarians preached love and peace. In a 1964 article in the daily newspaper, *Public Opinion*, one Rastafarian said: "A Rastaman can't bruk shop, a Rastaman can't chop up no one with machete,—Rastaman him no business with gun" (Heymans 8). In the *Star*, a Jamaican afternoon newspaper tabloid, Brother Aubrey Brown, a Rastafarian spokesperson, argued that the Rastafarian movement did not condone preaching "race hatred . . . against the pink nor the yellow" (qtd. in "Watch Word" 7). The *Report* of the UWI research team confirmed this nonviolent attitude when it reported that a "great majority of Ras Tafari brethren are peaceful citizens who do not believe in violence." The *Report* did suggest, however, that the movement was heterogeneous, and that a small minority of Rastafarians were criminals, revolutionaries, or "mentally deranged" (27). However, most Rastafarians did not seem to fit the Jamaican government's portrait of their cause as a violent, revolutionary social movement.

SKA AND THE ROOTS OF RASTAFARIAN PROTEST MUSIC

In the late 1950s, many Jamaicans loved American music. Jamaica's affection for U.S. musical forms reflected the worldwide dominance of the U.S. music industry and the fact that until the late 1950s Jamaica lacked its own recording industry. In a 1994 interview, Dermot Hussey, a former employee of the Jamaica Broadcasting Corporation (JBC) and Radio Jamaica Rediffusion Limited (RJR), noted that American music—big band, swing music, and jazz—had long been popular in Jamaica, and many Jamaicans believed foreign music was more "sophisticated" than their own indigenous forms. By the late 1950s, a new American music, rhythm and blues (R&B), had begun to captivate Jamaicans. While some R&B and rock-and-roll artists (such as Bill Haley and the Comets) played to cheering Jamaican audiences, most of the music was either brought back from the United States or heard on transistor radio from U.S. radio stations, such as WINZ in Miami, Florida (Witmer 15).

Early American R&B stars became role models for struggling young Jamaican musicians. Fats Domino was extremely popular in Jamaica because he "dealt with black life" (G. White, "Mento" 38). Early ska bands, such as the Wailers, even imitated the appearance of the R&B artists. Peter Tosh, one of the Wailers' founding members, recalled in the documentary *Caribbean Nights: The Bob Marley Story* that the "slick style" of short Afros, silk clothes, and sunglasses was adopted by ska bands hoping to "look like the ting." Recording under the direction of Clement "Sir Coxsone" Dodd in the two-track Studio One in Kingston, ska groups such as the Charmers and the Gaylands modeled themselves after the Impressions and the Platters, singing about sexual temptation, longing, and lost love. Some Jamaican groups, such as the Three Tops, even named themselves after American R&B stars in their efforts to emulate black American musical forms.

Even before the rise of ska, Jamaica had produced a generation of legendary jazz and big band musicians. According to Dermot Hussey:

14

> We had turned out a generation of musicians that were able to not only win acclaim here, but migrate to Britain primarily. People like Bertie King . . . established themselves also in the United States, and recorded for Blue Note records. So, there was this kind of level of musical excellence, particularly from the instrumental point of view. And that carried over into the ska period for a bit.

The popularity of this music was often credited to the influence of the Europeanized school missions in Jamaica. The Alpha Boys' School, a kind of reform school located in West Kingston, was the best example of how European schools of music were established in Jamaica to train Jamaican musicians to emulate the "European wind band tradition" (Witmer 12). The Alpha Boys' School sported an extraordinary music school and graduated some of Jamaica's finest big band, swing, and jazz instrumentalists. The Alpha Boys' School also trained musicians to fulfill national duties, such as playing for the Jamaica Military Band (Witmer 12).

The popularity of both R&B and ska was linked directly to a technology known in Jamaica as the "sound system." Sound systems were portable music systems on wheels; vans would carry high-fidelity playback equipment to neighborhood dances in Kingston (Winders 68). These gatherings usually took place in outdoor venues, such as neighborhood yards (Witmer 16). In order to provide this service, all that was needed was access to a power line. With an available power source, a sound system could envelope the community in music with two to eight speaker systems (Davis, "Talking Drums" 33).

The sound system promoted R&B, music typically unavailable to many Jamaicans. Legendary ska producer and promoter Clement Dodd often traveled to the United States and reentered Jamaica with copies of American recordings. The sound systems were instrumental in exposing Jamaicans to American music, because the "majority of Jamaicans then could not afford the radios that could pick up foreign stations, and so were not exposed to the kinds of music coming out of America. It was left to the sound-systems to educate and entertain the average Jamaican to the musical happenings" (Jingles 1).

More important, the sound system became the focal point for the development of a community of dissent. As one of the few affordable social activities for the poor, the sound system brought music to places where the voice of the poor could be heard without interference by local authorities. As cultural critic Dick Hebdige has written, the "sound-system came to represent, particularly for the young, a precious inner sanctum, uncontaminated by alien influences, a black heart beating back to Africa" (*Subculture* 38). At a sound-system gathering, a deejay encouraged dancing and made toasts to the audience.[5] Yet the deejay also would engage in a running commentary on political events in Jamaica.

By 1962, Jamaican ska was a hot musical item. A 1962 issue of *Spotlight Newsmagazine*, a Jamaican music magazine, reported that "whether or not it catches on in the States, there is no doubt that Ska is a big business in Jamaica" ("Ska—The Up Beat" 31–2). The ska sound (called "blue beat" in England) even created a national tremor in England. In "blue beat," the music's "monotonous, pulsating and compulsive" rhythms inspired a frenzied dance underscored by "the guttural grunts and groans of the dancers, who act like an exhausted person gasping for breath" (Patterson, "The Dance" 401). Edward Seaga, future JLP prime minister and a pioneer in recording Jamaican Revivalist music, managed to book a ska band at the 1964 World's Fair in New York. Despite ska's popularity, however, Jamaica's upper classes often ridiculed the music as an inferior art of the lower classes.

Protest Lyrics

Many ska songs were either searing, jazzy instrumentals or romantic love songs. Borrowing from the American black music tradition of jazz and blues, the theme of personal angst was materialized in ska lyrics that highlighted male-female relationships. Within these genres, especially the blues, women were portrayed as embodying love and loneliness, devotion and infidelity (Spencer 126). One might read some ska songs, such as the Checkmates' "Turn Me On" and Lee Perry's "Sugar Bag," as strictly "trivial" love songs (*Ska Bonanza*). In most of the songs, however, ska musicians expressed deep personal pain, brought about by the "corrupting" female influence. The temptation of female flesh and sexual pleasures ultimately led to "lonesome feelings," "teardrops," "broken hearts," and "lost love." The Wailers' "I Need You" found the dejected male "ashamed" of his "lost love." In order to fight from being a "small man" the victim declared: "I don't need you" (*One Love*). The woman thus became a symbol of only temporary pleasure, followed by hard luck, separation, and alienation.

However, many of the music's references—the social conditions of the ghetto, God as a redeemer, and repatriation to the "promised land"—clearly demonstrated ska's budding political concerns.

For example, ska musicians hinted at the brewing discontent of Jamaica's poor. In the shantytown, where an insult could quickly turn into a fatality, Bob Marley warned "Mr. Talkative" that too much gossip would lead to an early demise (*One Love*). Eric "Monty" Morris, an early ska musician, sang about a single mother raising children in poverty: "Old lady who live in a shoe / She had so many children / She didn't know what to do." Other artists, such as Theophilus Beckford, discussed the problem of youth in jail: "Georgie and the Old Shoes has gone to jail / Well if you're looking for poor Georgie / He's behind de [the] wall" (qtd. in G. White, "Mento" 41). Jamaican musician and record producer Prince Buster explored the issue of racial tension in the ghetto with the hit "Blackhead Chinee Man." The song was not just a direct attack against Derrick Morgan, a successful ska musician, but a warning about the potentially explosive conflict between "native" blacks and the foreign merchant class in Jamaica (Clarke 79). While calling attention to such social and political problems, however, ska stopped short of calling for rebellion. In 1963, the Wailers' first hit single, "Simmer Down," actually called upon Jamaicans to "cool" their tempers:

> *Simmer down, control your temper*
> *Simmer down and you'll get stronger*
> *Simmer down. Can't you hear what I say?*
> *Simmer down. Why don't you, why don't you*
> *Simmer down?* (One Love)

Ska musicians frequently looked to God for solace. Spirituals and gospel music had historical roots in a country populated with Christian churches. American gospel music has a direct link to the slave experience in the cotton fields. Gospel music draws on African tribal music, black spirituals, slave work songs, and Protestant church hymns (Carpenter 405). Gospel music has since influenced folk, blues, and R&B. In particular, the Wailers' string of gospel singles, including the songs "Amen" and "Habits," reflected the importance of the Christian church in the lives of many of these musicians (*One Love*).

As in most spirituals, God's role was that of a silent redeemer. As a "shining light" or "spirit," the faithful experienced God's presence and patiently waited for God to fulfill biblical prophecy. In "Over the River," the Jiving Juniors invoked the imagery of the Second Coming: "I'll be here when he come / My savior, my savior / I'll be here when he come" (*Ska Bonanza*). In the Wailers' song, "I Am Going Home," Bob Marley cried for God to "carry me home" (*One Love*). With God's will at work, the oppressed passively waited for liberation and deliverance.

The theme of repatriation to the "promised land" also can be located in a variety of ska songs. Despite the fact that ska musicians did not focus attention on the Rastafarian goal of returning to Africa, the repatriation motif was important in developing subsequent Rastafarian themes. Ska musicians associated biblical references to the River Jordan with the theme of returning home. In the Bible, the River Jordan stretched from the Sea of Galilee to the Dead Sea and symbolically represented the watery impasse between the wandering "lost" Jewish tribe and the promised land. Over the opening chords of the Wailers' "I Am Going Home," Bob Marley sang of the River Jordan while the background vocals cried, "I am going home." In another ska song, "River Jordan," Clancy Eccles's backup vocalists repeated the chorus "roll River Jordan roll," while Eccles described Noah's Ark, thunderous rain, and God's return to rescue the faithful from oppression (*Tougher Than Tough*). Although the Maytals' "Six and Seven Books of Moses" simply recited the books of the Old Testament, the song hinted at the Israelites' return to the promised land (*Tougher Than Tough*).

In one of the few ska songs to employ Rastafarian images explicitly, "Carry Go Bring Come," Justin Hines and the Dominoes invoked the image of Mount Zion, an image that would echo through reggae songs during the 1970s. In the song, Hines alerted followers to "seek in Mount Zion high / Instead of keeping oppression upon an innocent man" (*Tougher Than Tough*).

While some ska songs hinted at repatriation "back home," "Carry Go Bring Come" discussed the oppressive experience in Jamaica and specifically acknowledged Mount Zion in Africa as the promised land. Although the ska sound was mostly a blend of several genres of popular music, Rastafarian themes were clearly expressed in song titles and instrumentation.

Musical Instrumentation

Ska music blended a variety of musical styles. Kenneth M. Bilby, a scholar of Jamaican music, has referred to the blending of musical styles as the process of creolization. Creolization refers to a "meeting and blending of two or more older traditions on new soil, and a subsequent elaboration of form" ("The Caribbean" 2). American musical forms such as jazz and big band music inspired ska's horn sound, and R&B influenced the music's guitar style, the types of chords used, and the length of the song (usually under four minutes). Jamaican music expert Garth White has also suggested that ska was influenced by its predecessor, mento: ska's "shuffle-rhythm [is] close to mento but even closer to the backbeat of the r&b" ("Mento" 38).[6] Ska also contained a mix of blues and African elements such as call and response (Turner 148).

Ska's top music producers, Clement Dodd, Leslie Kong, and Duke Reid, would invite young, upstart ska musicians like Jimmy Cliff to record songs with a studio "house band," consisting of some of the best musicians on the island. Because of the limitations of two-track recording, a producer would be forced to record the band "live" (i.e., all the musicians would play in the same room at the same time). One of Jamaica's most influential bass guitarists, Jackie Jackson, recalled the limitations of the two-track studio:

> It was all of the instruments on one track and the vocals on the other. Thank the Lord 4-track came along. You used to play out your

soul on 2-track because every time you take a cut, all of the instruments pop up on one track. Sometimes you go back and listen and you can't hear something. So you take another cut, you go back in and listen, and now something too *loud*. It went on like that for ever and ever because there was no separation. (qtd. in Gorney 41)

Although the limitations of the recording technology played a significant role in the often uneven and "raw" production, ska songs clearly reflected the joyful celebration of independence and the bustling urban life of West Kingston. And the music's relatively fast tempo accounted in large measure for ska's joyful sound. Compared to reggae music of the 1970s (averaging approximately 72 beats per minute [bpm]), ska songs achieved a faster tempo of approximately 110 to 130 beats per minute. Songs such as the Wailers' "Simmer Down" (124 bpm), Justin Hines and the Dominoes' "Carry Go Bring Come" (126 bpm), the Skatalites' "Nimble Foot Ska" (128 bpm), and Don Drummond and Roland Alphonso's "Roll On Sweet Don (Heaven and Hell)" (131 bpm) exemplified ska's quick, often festive, beat.7

Like most western music, ska music was played in 4/4 or common time (four quarter notes per bar).[8] The ska ensemble included a rhythm guitar and, occasionally, a lead guitar, an upright bass, drums, lead and harmony vocals, and often an extensive horn section that included a trombone, trumpet, and a tenor or alto saxophone (or both). Unlike later rocksteady and reggae bands, a ten-piece ska band took on the appearance of a large jazz ensemble or a big band.

Although ska borrowed heavily from other musical genres, the musicians created a unique rhythmic sound and style. In the early 1960s, ska singer and producer Prince Buster asked his guitarist Jah Jerry to emphasize the offbeat in an attempt to move ska beyond simply copying the R&B sound (Barrow 11). In most American popular music, the rhythm guitar accented the downbeat or played on the underlined numbers: (1 & 2 & 3 & 4 &). In contrast, ska guitarists played on the offbeat or the "and" (1 & 2 & 3 & 4 &). The guitarist's emphasis on the offbeat, rather than the downbeat, created the distinctive sound that has since characterized all of Jamaica's popular music.

In the typical ska arrangement, the piano and horns would help the guitarist emphasize ska's offbeat sound. For example, Don Drummond's instrumental, "Man in the Street," featured a guitar, piano, and horns playing the same rhythm, each instrument emphasizing the offbeat. However, in songs such as Derrick Morgan's "Forward March," when a guitarist was not available, the horns and piano provided the offbeat pattern (*Tougher Than Tough*).

As a musical experience, the rhythm guitar created a positive, almost optimistic sound. The ability of the guitarist to create this "happy" and "uplifting" sound was a result of the usage of major, as opposed to minor, chords and keys. For centuries, western musicians have used major chords and keys to convey "happy" and "optimistic" feelings to listeners. Although some ska songs did utilize minor keys, most songs were written in major keys, relying on the three major or primary chords (I, IV, V). Playing a short, choppy rhythm, the ska guitarist enhanced this "happy" sound by playing mid-register voicings on the top three or four smallest strings near the middle of the guitar neck. Some guitarists further emphasized this sound by employing more frequent chord changes. In "Simmer Down," the guitarist used two chords, changing every two beats (1 & 2 & 3 & 4 &) within the 4/4 framework.

While the rhythm guitar, piano, and horn section anchored ska's offbeat sound, the drummer typically emphasized downbeats 2 and 4. The drummer typically played a timekeeping role, utilizing only a minimal number of percussive instruments: snare drum, hi-hat, ride cymbal and, occasionally, the bass drum. In most ska songs, the drummer would hit the snare drum on beats 2 and 4, while playing a steady eighth-note pattern on the hi-hat or a ride cymbal. Yet, in songs such as "Man in the Street" and "Nimble Foot Ska" (*Ska Bonanza*) the drummer played a more adventurous role, using bass drum accents, snare fills, and busier improvisational work on the hi-hat to add color to the sound. Despite these occasional rhythmic flourishes, the drummer played a subordinate role in the ska arrangement. It was not until the birth of international reggae that the drums became an extremely important, if not dominant, musical instrument.

The bass, along with the rhythm guitar and drums, served as an important part of ska's percussive sound. Employing a stand-up bass (electric bass guitars were not widely used in Jamaica until the mid-1960s), the ska bassist would frequently play a "walking" bass line, a bass figure often heard on jazz and blues records. To achieve this sound, the bassist would play four quarter notes per bar illustrating the "one-note-per-beat" style. For example, in Jimmy Cliff's 1962 song "Miss Jamaica" (*Tougher Than Tough*), the bass player played this ska bass line (figure 1.1):

A simplified version of this bass rhythm would look like this (figure 1.2):

X	X	X	X
Beat 1	Beat 2	Beat 3	Beat 4

While the electric guitar, piano, upright bass, and drums functioned as ska's unwavering rhythmic "heartbeat," the horn section would have far more latitude and freedom to explore the boundaries and scope of its collective function and sound. The horn section performed multiple roles, including sustaining chord tones, doubling the guitar's offbeat staccato chords, playing a song's main riff or theme, and—at times—even improvising solo passages. For example, in "Carry Go Bring Come" the trombone provided the opening statement, while additional horns acted in a supportive manner by blowing unison lines in the background. After a four-bar theme, the trombone joined the other horns, and for the remainder of the song, the tenor sax, trumpet, and trombone played in unison, while additional horns doubled the guitar's offbeat figure. In this song, one horn section functioned harmonically and rhythmically by doubling the offbeat guitar chords, while the other horns played a unison melody.

Frequently, ska songs such as "Nimble Foot Ska" featured complicated horn arrangements. In this song, after the drummer provided a brief introductory snare fill, the tenor sax introduced the song's eight-bar theme before the rest of the horn section (trombone, alto sax, and trumpet) entered with a well-structured background theme. Early in the song, the horn section played a harmonized theme, while the tenor sax improvised a brief solo. As the song progressed, a horn trio consisting of trumpet, trombone, and sax alternated between playing harmony and unison lines. Similar to many early ska songs, "Nimble Foot Ska" demonstrated the genre's reliance on horns and the complexity of these arrangements.

Ska songs would also include another important "instrument," the human voice. Typically, ska songs featured a lead vocal and two or three backup singers. While most vocal arrangements were fairly rudimentary, some songs previewed the more complex vocal arrangements that would be heard in future rocksteady and reggae songs. In the Jiving Juniors' song "Over the River," for example, the lead singer and three backup singers harmonized during the song's introduction. As the song shifted into the chorus, the backup singers vocalized the phrase "I'll be here when he come," while the lead singer repeated the words "over the river." Later in the song, the two vocal parts switched roles: the backup singers repeated "over the river" while the lead singer enthusiastically proclaimed: "I'll be here when he come." Despite vocal workouts like "Over the River," which reflected a type of call-and-response approach, most ska songs employed more basic vocal arrangements such as a lead vocal and backup harmony parts.

In sum, even though the ska sound was heavily dominated by the accented offbeat, it also exploited the tension between the offbeat and the downbeat. While the electric guitar, piano, and occasionally one or more horns emphasized the offbeat, the drums and the bass anchored the downbeat. Another important characteristic of the ska sound was the combination of structured repetition and improvisation. The electric guitar, bass, piano, and drums played with very little variation; in comparison, one or more horns and, occasionally, the vocals would improvise "around" the rest of the ensemble to help create ska's "happy," "joyous," and "uplifting" sound. Some of these vocal arrangements harkened back to traditional American black music, especially gospel music, which is often marked by vocal improvisations. Perhaps ska can best be characterized as a product of creolization, borrowing heavily from black American music (jazz, gospel, and R&B), while also incorporating indigenous (mento) and African elements into its sound. In addition, ska music began to reflect the influence of the Rastafarian movement.

The connection between Rastafari and ska music was most evident in the work of two pioneering musicians: Oswald Williams, popularly known as "Count Ossie," and Don Drummond. In the 1940s, Count Ossie was inspired by Burru drumming, an African drumming pattern, and he established several Rastafarian camps and invited many sympathetic to the Rastafarian movement to be part of his musical experiments (G. White, "Mento" 39). His earliest recordings have not survived, but Ossie highlighted Rastafarian drumming in the haunting song "Oh Carolina" (*Tougher Than Tough*). The song was sung by the Folkes Brothers with Count Ossie and other Rastafarian musicians adding traditional Rastafarian drumming and backup vocals.

Rastafarian influences were also evident in the titles of his instrumental songs such as "Another Moses" and "Babylon Gone." "Another Moses" referred cryptically to the divinity of Haile Selassie, and "Babylon Gone" expressed the Rastafarian hope in being delivered from Jamaica's oppressive social structure to their home in Africa (G. White, "The Development" 64). In the mid-1960s, Ossie formed a group called the Mystic Revelation of Rastafari. Cedric Brooks, a noted Jamaican musician, said that "Count Ossie was the pioneer in bringing the Rasta Music into the open" (Brooks 14).

Don Drummond has been credited with introducing Rastafarian influences into the musical nucleus of ska. As the leading trombonist for the Skatalites, Drummond's songs—"Tribute to Marcus Garvey," "Reincarnation," and "The Return of Paul Bogle"—reflected his Rastafarian faith (Jerry 1). Dermot Hussey explained in an interview the connection between Drummond and Rastafarian themes: "If you noticed all the themes that had an African orientation in ska music, "Don de Lion," "Father East," . . . all those things, he was the one that I think that had a great association with the kind of Rastafarian sensibility."

In 1965, Drummond, who had a history of mental illness, murdered his girlfriend, and in 1969 he committed suicide in a Jamaican asylum. The black nationalist newspaper, *Abeng*, mourned Drummond's death and praised his contribution to ska. One Rastafarian writer, Bongo Jerry, characterized Drummond as the "melody of Freedom Sounds." Recognizing Drummond's incredible musical skill and tragic life, Jerry confessed: "[W]e hurt inside when we remember that he was pushed around, pushed about and then finally shoved out by Babylon" (1).

The influence of Count Ossie and Don Drummond created the opportunity for ska musicians to enter Rastafarian camps, to engage in musical experiments, and to become sensitive to the Rastafarian ethos. Because of their association with the movement, these musicians were "always kept under surveillance by the police" (Clarke 67). In effect, the fusion of ska and Rastafari initiated the process of creating a musical community unified against an oppressive social system.

By the mid-1960s, however, Jamaica's popular music would evolve into rocksteady, a more aggressive, more politically minded protest music. Although not politically explicit protest music, ska initiated this evolution of Jamaican popular music toward a message of dissent against repression, intolerance, and discrimination.

Chapter Two

ROCKSTEADY, THE RUDE BOY, AND THE POLITICAL AWAKENING OF RASTAFARI

> Rude bwoy [boy] is that person, native, who is totally disenchanted with
> the ruling system; who generally is descended from the "African" elements in
> the lower class and who is now armed with ratchets (German made knives),
> other cutting instruments and with increasing frequency nowadays, with guns
> and explosives.
>
> —**Garth White**

In the mid-1960s, Jamaica's tenuous national unity began to crumble
into political instability and social chaos. The island continued to suffer
from economic dependence on foreign countries, trade imbalances, rising
unemployment, land displacement, and shortages of housing and food. The
economic boom of the 1960s continued to benefit Jamaica's elite, as the
wealthy classes drove shiny new imported American cars and protected
their homes from crime with electric fences and snarling attack dogs. In
stark contrast, the poor survived in West Kingston's "blazing" war zone of

26

cardboard shacks, human waste, and steel-gray cement factories (Patterson, *Children* 17–27).

As Jamaica's social conditions continued to deteriorate, protest groups increasingly defied the political leadership of the dominant classes. The Rastafarians declared their racial pride more openly, while rebellious young toughs in Kingston's slums coalesced into what became known as the Rude Boy youth rebellion. The Jamaica Council for Human Rights (JCHR), a small group of lawyers, formed in late 1967 and committed itself to the goal of defending the human rights of all Jamaicans (Gray 144–9). The growing line of resistance in Jamaica reflected the poor's "bold assertion of a black radical consciousness [that] challenged the political and moral leadership of the dominant classes" (Gray 115).

This black radical consciousness was, in part, inspired by the proliferation of liberation movements around the world. In the United States, the black Muslims became an increasingly threatening symbol of defiance against white America. U.S. black radicals Stokely Carmichael and Eldridge Cleaver broke off from the New Left and became members of, among other organizations, the Black Panthers. In Africa and Asia, national liberation movements challenged European colonial control. Fidel Castro's successful socialist revolution in Cuba brought this revolutionary impulse to the Caribbean. Sociologists George Beckford and Michael Witter, in *Small Garden . . . Bitter Weed: The Political Economy of Struggle and Change in Jamaica*, claimed that Jamaica's lower classes were influenced by all of these developments and believed that they were part of a worldwide movement seeking liberation from colonial rule (76).

The Jamaica Labour Party (JLP) responded to this increased agitation with repressive measures. After incidents of civil unrest increased in 1965, the government allocated more funding to bolster the police force in lieu of improving health-care services (Munroe 199). To protect its political power, the JLP tried to maintain Britain's neo-colonial social stratification system, keeping whites at the top and blacks at the bottom of the socioeconomic structure. The JLP continued to support property owners and foreign interests, while neglecting small Jamaican-owned businesses and the growing numbers of unemployed youth

(Beckford and Witter 83). The JLP continued to rely on "restrictive laws and unilateral, nonreviewable edicts to maintain its rule" (Gray 196).

During this time, a new genre of Jamaican popular music, rocksteady, expressed more clearly the problems and contradictions of Jamaican life. Most popular critics and music scholars recognized rocksteady as a more politically aggressive protest music than ska. Jamaican music scholar Verena Reckord observed that rocksteady musicians "were coming to grips with the stifling social conditions which pervaded life in the ghetto, from which most of them came" (11). Patrick Hylton claimed that rocksteady musicians sang "songs that were expressive of the people's suffering, their everyday life, and their attitude towards the society in which they live[d]" (27). Longtime reggae observer Garth White has commented that rocksteady built cultural solidarity with its "qualities of rugged morality" and "fearless protest," qualities that later would characterize reggae as well ("Mento" 42). Clearly, rocksteady represented a leap forward in the development of a popular music as a means of social protest in Jamaica.

At the same time, while most Rastafarians continued to espouse nonviolence and were politically apathetic, the movement began to gain some popularity among more politically active middle-class youths. In 1966, Haile Selassie proposed a change in the movement's repatriation plan, calling for members of the movement to liberate the Jamaican people before returning to Africa (Barrett 160). This doctrinal change provided the ideological space for Rastafarians to become more politically active in Jamaica. Reflecting these changes, rocksteady was clearly a more aggressive and politically minded protest music than ska. While rocksteady echoed ska's mournings of lost love and its reflections upon the misery of living in the unbearable shantytowns of West Kingston, the music also immortalized the gun-toting Rude Boy, condemned the police officer and the judge as symbols of oppression, and emphasized to a greater degree the Rastafarian themes of racial pride and repatriation. This tension between the personal and the political, between passivity and activism, and between peace and violence identified rocksteady as something of a transitional form between ska and the explicitly political reggae of the 1970s.

JAMAICA: FROM INDEPENDENCE TO SOCIAL PROTEST

For the thousands sandwiched in the shacks of West Kingston, independence did not significantly change Jamaica's social and political conditions. As the prospects for the poor to achieve employment, education, or even decent housing became more of a distant dream, Jamaica experienced growing political strife: gang warfare, riots, strikes, and increases in crime. In this increasingly tense political climate, "the rulers [were] afraid of the black masses and the latter angry and alienated" (Brodber, "Socio-cultural" 62).

The government and the poor clashed over several issues during this period. In October 1963, the JLP initiated "Operation Shantytown," ordering the destruction of shantytowns in the Kingston Pen area and other areas in West Kingston in order to build an industrial complex, an Esso Oil refinery, and new housing projects (Gray 119). JLP minister of housing, D. Clement Tavares, told the *Daily Gleaner* that the slum clearing project was necessary to "provide a new and model township in the area" ("Agitators" 2). This effort was expanded in February 1966 when riot police charged into two West Kingston slums, the Payne Avenue and Majesty Pen areas, and displaced more than five hundred slum dwellers and their children (Gray 119–20). Nearly five months later, on July 12, 1966, the bulldozers returned to displace nearly fifteen hundred more residents. This led to squatters "scamper[ing] back and forth to secure spots, hurrying to clear out their belongings as the bulldozers' shovels loomed" ("Bulldozers" 1). In a critical overview of the JLP's slum-clearing policies in the 1960s, political scientist Obika Gray has argued that the JLP's "modernization" project was, in fact, an attempt to strike back at the militant poor, establish Tivoli Gardens as a political stronghold of JLP supporters, and continue the expansion of industry to benefit local and foreign capital (119).

While the shantytowns of West Kingston were transformed into rubble, civil unrest spread throughout the island. In 1965, "anti-Chinese" riots broke out after a Chinese store owner allegedly beat his black clerk (Brodber, "Socio-cultural" 62). During the three-day riot, the police arrested eighty-six protestors, while youths looted Chinese stores and intimidated store owners ("City Getting" 1). In the same year, sugar workers from the Frome and Monymusk sugar estates threw down their machetes and went on strike. The West Indies Sugar Company (WISCO) had failed to pay these workers their traditional bonuses (Gray 109).

Gang warfare in West Kingston contributed to the civil unrest in Jamaica. In particular, gang warfare between supporters of the JLP and the PNP increased. By 1966, the hiring of ghetto gang members as political thugs had become commonplace, as officials for both political parties "began to legitimize the role of the gunman as an *enforcer* in their rivalry, thereby investing an anomic figure with a decisive role in national politics" (Gray 120). Gang members would be hired for handouts or promises of a job and trained in sharpshooting or intimidation tactics. In the fall of 1966, the political warfare became so intense the JLP was forced to call a state of emergency for three weeks. The *Gleaner* reported that West Kingston had been transformed into an "armed camp" ("State of Emergency" 1).

Writing in the *New World Quarterly*, political scientist Douglas Hall summarized the thinking behind Jamaica's web of politics and violence: "Vote for me and you might get a job. Vote for my opponent and, if I win, you probably won't. Harass my opponent in his electoral campaign and get a hand-out for a meal" (13). In addition, those arrested could look to the politicians they supported to get them back on the street. In 1966, the *Daily Gleaner* editorialized against the politicians who bailed their supporters out of jail:

> No wonder these criminal pests have been going around the suburbs as well as the slums behaving like new lords of the jungle! They knew that, more often than not, just as soon as they were arrested, some politician would be behind the scenes sending to bail them. ("At Last" 1)

Many of these "criminal pests" were rebellious ghetto youths, called Rude Boys or "Rudies." The product of the mass migration from rural areas to the city streets, the Rude Boys began to appear in the Kingston slums in 1961. By the beginning of 1965, the Rude Boys had become a more unified and organized youth rebellion. Ranging in age from fourteen to twenty-five,

Rude Boys were gangs of "discontented" Jamaican youths who carried knives, cutlasses, and guns (Kaslow 12). They lived to "run faster or jump higher or fuck longer or smoke more dope" than anybody else (Boot and Thomas 38). Rude Boys embraced the image of an outlaw hero, breaking all the rules yet struggling against the forces of evil and oppression. Writing in a 1967 issue of *Caribbean Quarterly*, Garth White's article "Rudie, Oh Rudie!" described the Rude Boys' enemy: the whole middle class. The Rude Boys' anger and violence was "pointed not only against the settler and his descendants, but also to all that class of persons who occupy the middle rung in the society" (39).

The Rude Boys' taste for intimidation, looting, and guns was a direct threat to the safety of the middle class. The Rude Boys also inverted middle-class values, distinguishing themselves with unkempt hair, untucked shirts, and working-class speech idioms (Gray 73). Because the Rude Boys rejected the values of the middle and upper classes, their activities became synonymous with political opposition to the JLP (Gray 117). The Rude Boys became a defiant symbol of a new generation opposed to the arrogance of the middle class and to a political and economic system that produced unemployment and poverty.

Jamaican citizens and police officers often associated the Rude Boys' antisocial behavior with the Rastafarians' insolent display of racial pride. And because some Rude Boys adopted the Rastafarian style, sporting dreadlocks and muttering the movement's unique vocabulary, the Rastafarians' image of a "violent cult" was further accentuated (Campbell, *Rasta* 111). In addition, many of Jamaica's unemployed youth (i.e., Rude Boys, gang members) claimed to be Rastafarians. In his study of the Park youth gang, located in West Kingston, anthropologist Barry Chevannes observed that many of the gang members who supposedly embraced Rastafari were not "concerned with the niceties and subtleties of Rastafari doctrine and ritual" ("Rastafari" 421). Instead, many of the members embraced Rastafari because the movement was an intrinsic part of the social milieu of the ghetto ("The Rastafari" 398).

In more significant ways, however, Rude Boys and Rastafarians espoused two radically different ideologies. Rude Boys did not generally share the

Rastafarians' religious training, faith in biblical prophecy, or desires for repatriation to Africa. In turn, most Rastafarians did not agree with the Rude Boys' use of violence, their desire for material prosperity, and their embrace of American culture (Gray 74–5). While Rastafarians assumed the moral leadership of the ghetto, living an ascetic and restrained lifestyle of meditation and personal reflection, the Rude Boys reveled in materialism and violence. In short, as Obika Gray has summarized the difference, the "militant youths stopped short of a thoroughgoing embrace of Rastafarian ideology" (74).

Jamaica's deepening economic crisis and the JLP's continued autocratic rule encouraged protest by Jamaica's lower classes. Faced with the destruction of their shantytowns and increased gang warfare, the Rude Boy became a particularly violent symbol of the poor's resistance against economic exploitation and inequality. Although the Rude Boys and the Rastafarian movement shared an anti-colonialist policy, the two groups promoted distinct solutions to solve Jamaica's social and political problems. Nevertheless, Haile Selassie's doctrinal change on repatriation created the possibility for more common ground between the Rude Boys and the Rastafarians.

THE RASTAFARIAN MOVEMENT: LIBERATION BEFORE REPATRIATION

While the Rude Boys struck terror into the hearts of the middle class, most Rastafarians retreated in a different direction. By 1965, most Rastafarians still advocated political disengagement, believing that their salvation would come from "entailed meditation, discussion, and reading the Bible" (Gray 74). Many Rastafarians were waiting for Haile Selassie to send his ships to the shores of Jamaica to take the oppressed away to Ethiopia. Yet, by the end of 1967, more and more middle-class youth were beginning to find the Rastafarian movement appealing, and the visit of Haile Selassie increased the political consciousness of the Rastafarian movement.

Most middle-class and upper-class Jamaicans viewed the Rastafarian movement with contempt. In response, Rastafarian spokespersons attempted to overcome misconceptions about the movement. In a "Treatise on the

Rastafarian Movement," published in 1966, Samuel Elisha Brown, a Rastafarian spokesperson, noted that Rastafarians were vegetarians, worshiped
Haile Selassie, and respected the "brotherhood of mankind." Throughout
the article, Brown stressed that Rastafarians "shall right all wrongs and
bring ease to the suffering bodies," and that the movement possessed "the
key to war and peace in the Universe" (39–40). In that same year, Brown
wrote a letter to the *Gleaner* complaining that Rastafarians have been marginalized within Jamaican society "because of his refusal to forget his
[African] origin" (10).

Stigmatized as a "cult of outcasts," the Rastafarian movement nevertheless began attracting more attention because of the growing consciousness
among Jamaican blacks of their African heritage. The Rastafarians' appeal
slowly spread into middle-class neighborhoods, as young blacks became
"sensitive to their ambiguous place in a sharply divided society" and to
aspects of white culture that had "served to alienate them from the black
masses" (Beckford and Witter 77). Declaring Jamaican folk hero Marcus
Garvey a prophet and embracing African nationalism, the Rastafarians
stimulated "popular remembrances and resentments in a way that others in
the society could not." As Obika Gray summarized the Rastafarians' appeal
in the mid-1960s: "No other ideology or group appeared capable of com-
peting with them" (146).

In 1966, the Rastafarian movement gained still more public notice with
the arrival of Haile Selassie, who visited Jamaica by invitation of the
Jamaican government. In effect, Selassie's visit "persuaded some political
leaders that the Rastas could no longer be written off as dangerous freaks"
(Plummer 21). On the day of his arrival, Selassie was greeted by an esti-
mated crowd of 100,000, about 10,000 of whom were Rastafarians. Many
Rastafarians crowded around the plane, chanting, praying, and smoking
from waterpipes filled with ganja. Writing in a 1967 issue of *Caribbean
Quarterly*, Rastafarian journalist and poet Ras Dizzy I. recalled the arrival of
Selassie in Jamaica:

> The King of Kings arrived at the Palisadoes Airport at about ten min-
> utes past one in the afternoon. Many thousands of well-wishers shouted in

honour of His Imperial Majesty and his family. It might here be mentioned that the black multitude of Israel went to receive the visit of their King and the white folks went to look into the Negus' face and then to decide which God they will serve. . . . As soon as the Negus had entered the airport then, my God His Majesty wept. The King wept after seeing the thousands of Rastafarians and the accompanying multitude of black people who had come to give voice to the slogans for repatriation back to Ethiopia. ("The Rastas Speak" 41)

Before the mid-1960s, many Rastafarians believed that liberation could be realized only through a physical repatriation to Africa. During his only trip to Jamaica, however, Selassie proposed a new concept of repatriation. After Selassie allegedly met with several Rastafari leaders, a new tenet of repatriation emerged: Rastafarians should liberate the Jamaican people before repatriation to Africa (Barrett 160). Some writers have claimed that Selassie's apparent change on repatriation inaugurated a new wave, in which the movement's apolitical philosophy gave way to more immediate, more political demands (Jacobs 87). This new political philosophy created, in turn, a division between "political" and "religious" Rastafarians.

From its inception, however, the Rastafarian movement was a mixture of both religious and political elements. Rastafarians were certainly "political" in that they claim African citizenship, openly expressed their racial pride, and argued that Jamaica's independence from Great Britain was a "farce" (de Albuquerque, "The Future" 24). Moreover, Rastafarians critiqued the "prevalent individualis[m]" and "imperialistic capitalism" that were responsible for the "African slave trade" and subsequent "massive poverty." However, anthropologist Yoshiko S. Nagashima distinguished "political" Rastafarians from their "religious" counterparts in terms of active political involvement in Jamaica. Thus, Rastafarian groups such as the Rastafarian Movement Association (RMA) were considered "political" in that they argued for active involvement in Jamaican politics. Religious Rastafarians, on the other hand, maintained that the movement must refuse to "participate in Jamaican politics as they have often felt betrayed" (2). In short, while political Rastafarians argued that active engagement in Jamaican politics would "provide them with authority and power to improve their living conditions," religious Rastafarians believed in the "depoliticisation of the Rastafarian movement" (Nagashima 31).

By early 1968, the new JLP government, led by Hugh Shearer, had become convinced that the growing political consciousness of the Rastafarian movement posed a threat to Jamaica's national security. In three separate raids, between January and June 1968, riot police and soldiers raided the headquarters of the notorious Rastafarian leader Claudius Henry, who had just formed a new group called the New Creation Peacemakers Association (NCPA) (Gray 149). In an editorial in the *Gleaner*, the Jamaica Council for Human Rights graphically recounted the brutal tactics employed during the raid. The JCHR alleged that police had illegally detained members, pointed rifles at children, destroyed food, and illegally seized personal property (14). By the summer of 1968, the JLP had more problems to deal with than Henry's supposed exploits. Dissent was spreading well beyond the Rastafarian community, aided in no small measure by the new music known as rocksteady.

ROCKSTEADY: THE AGGRESSIVE TURN IN JAMAICAN MUSIC

By 1965, ska musicians had begun moving away from the sounds of R&B and jazz. These musicians embraced a more emotional and direct form of U.S. black music, soul music. Born out of the American South, soul music was the product of a fusion of rock-and-roll, gospel, and R&B and blues. Stax records, in Memphis, Tennessee, was one of the major producers/recording studios of this new musical genre. The urgency of rock-and-roll transformed rhythm and blues into a more emotional, grittier, stripped-down music. Soul music was primarily characterized by the emergence of more emotional vocals and more insistent, bracing rhythms (Gillett 274). Rocksteady's attention to vocal harmonies and slower rhythms mirrored its American counterpart's new developments. In addition, rocksteady musicians recorded a number of American soul songs, such as Wilson Pickett's "In the Midnight Hour."

Music critics have suggested other reasons for the emergence of rock-steady. Some suggest that the "torpid steamy summer" of 1966 created a sit-uation in which "people no longer wanted to dance as frenetically as they had before" (Steffens, "Skatalites" 894). "Dizzy" Johnny Moore, a trumpeter for the Skatalites, argued that ska's decline was due to the inability of younger, less talented musicians to master the more difficult style of ska: "[Rocksteady] was really a slowing down of the beat and this was because the younger musicians, who were less knowledgeable about other forms of music than us, found it difficult to keep that fast ska beat" (qtd. in B. Henry 4).

Rocksteady never produced a dance craze like the "Ska Jerk." It did, however, assume a more rebellious stance, which explains why the Jamaican government did not market the music overseas. The rocksteady genre relied less on gospel and spiritual forms and more on the beliefs and feeling of Jamaica's disaffected classes. Like the name, the music was "steadier" and "rockier," but it also was "ruder" and more political.

Protest Lyrics

Many rocksteady and ska musicians were united in representing the frus-trations of the lower classes in Jamaica. Many of these musicians were poor, lower-class blacks who lived in the impoverished areas of West Kingston and struggled daily to overcome the lack of shelter, food, and steady employ-ment. Ska and rocksteady musicians acted as a musical community of dis-sent, and certainly both involved Rastafarians and those sympathetic to the movement.

Like ska, rocksteady featured "crying" as a common theme. Yet rock-steady musicians started to redirect this feeling from the personal pain of lost love to encompass the suffering experienced in the ghetto. In Alton and the Flames' "Cry Tough," the singer urged Jamaica's ghetto dwellers to stay tough, even when they grew old: "Cry tough / Don't you know you're slow? / Cry tough / You are getting old / How can a man be tough? / Tougher than the world / For if he's rough / He's against the world" (*Duke Reid's*). In U-Roy's song, "Everybody Bawling," the themes of pain and sadness grew out of the problems of separation, alienation, and poverty, as U-Roy cried,

"Everyone bawling / Crying out for love" (*Duke Reid's*). In the Three Tops' "It's Raining," the trio of voices sounded the theme of despair over the lack of food and shelter. Lamenting his bad luck and inability to find a direction in life, the singer decried a social situation where "you can't find your food or shoes" (*Duke Reid's*). To prove rocksteady's commitment to Jamaica's poor, the Wailers released an adaptation of Bob Dylan's song "Like a Rolling Stone." As the guitars jangled, Bob Marley sang familiar lyrics with special meaning in Jamaica: "How does it feel to be on your own / With no direction home / Like a complete unknown / Like a Rolling Stone" (*One Love*).

Unlike ska, however, rocksteady songs celebrated the rebel, memorializing the Rude Boy as a violent hero who sought "social" and "political" justice with a knife and a gun. While the Jamaican government publicly denounced the Rude Boy's violence and antisocial behavior, many rocksteady musicians championed the "good Rudie" by celebrating his strength, youth, intelligence, and aggressiveness. In one of the first songs to celebrate the Rude Boy, the Wailers' "Hooligan," the Rude Boy was portrayed as a violent disrupter of middle-class society. In the song, a Rude Boy visited the home of a love interest only to offend the household with his "dirty mouth" and "sharp studs." Upon his exit, the mother was "weeping" and the floor "covered with broken glass" (*One Love*). In the Wailers' "Let Him Go," Bunny Wailer reminded police authorities that the Rude Boy was "younger" and "smarter" and less mortal than ordinary Jamaicans (*One Love*). The Rude Boy became the "dangerous Rudie," the "stepping razor," and the "youthful hooligan" who resisted police enforcement, broke beer bottles at local dances, and wielded knives at middle-class Jamaicans on the dangerous Kingston streets.

Rocksteady musicians even celebrated the Rude Boys' penchant for guns. Baba Brooks's "Gun Fever" described newspaper headlines detailing a night of gunfire, fresh killings, and escape from the law. The Rude Boy, Brooks sang, had created a gun "fever" on this "little island" (qtd. in Waters 69). Prince Buster's "Too Hot" cautioned those who might combat the Rude Boy, warning that the Rude Boy, unwilling to give up his "guns," was "[p]ound for pound" "ruder" than his opposition. Those who tangled with the Rude Boy were advised to purchase "insurance" and to make out a "will" (qtd. in Hebdige, *Cut* 73).

As portrayed in rocksteady, the Rude Boys were so "rude" and "tough" that they deliberately clashed with police. In Desmond Dekker's "007 (Shanty Town)," a Rude Boy recently released from jail returned to his usual behavior of petty crime and murder in a joyous celebration, a "wail." As the Rude Boy fought "taller" police and "longer" soldiers, he was "weeping and a wailing" in defeat (*Tougher Than Tough*). The Wailers' song "Jailhouse," however, suggested that the Rude Boys might ultimately prevail over police repression. As the song ended, the police officer's baton grew "smaller" as the Rudie Boy grew "larger" (*One Love*). Rocksteady songs thus depicted Rude Boys' suffering at the hands of the police, but they also celebrated the Rude Boys' triumphs over law enforcement.

Rocksteady musicians also commented on the Rude Boys' problems with the judicial system, as symbolized by the figure, "the judge." The judge figure appeared in Prince Buster's "Judge Dread." In Rastafarian vocabulary, the word "dread" meant anyone who was "serious," "proud," or "feared." In the song "Judge Dread," a towering Rastafarian figure, Judge Dread, mindlessly sentenced Rude Boys to whippings, hard labor, and jail time. But to demonstrate the emerging alliance between the Rastafarian and the Rude Boy, Prince Buster's follow-up, "Barrister Pardon," had Judge Dread reversing his decision and granting the Rude Boys a pardon. As the song concluded, Judge Dread and the freed Rude Boys celebrated the pardon (Hebdige, *Cut* 73).

In another example, Derrick Morgan's "Tougher Than Tough," the judge publicly condemned some violent Rude Boys in court. The Rude Boys responded in unison, proclaiming that they did not "fear" incarceration because they were "strong as a lion" and "like iron" (*Tougher Than Tough*). As the song closed, the judge, apparently impressed with the Rude Boys' fearlessness, "set Rudie free."

These songs provided a revealing insight into the tenuous relationship between the Rastafarian and the Rude Boy. In "Judge Dread," the judge's moral decision to condemn the Rude Boys to imprisonment demonstrated the Rastafarians' rejection of violence. In "Barrister Pardon" and "Tougher Than Tough," however, the judge's decision to pardon the Rude Boys illustrated the turn from rejecting violence to condoning more aggressive protest against oppression in Jamaica.

While sending such mixed messages about the violence of the Rude Boys, rocksteady musicians continued to represent God as the invisible caretaker. Whether lamenting a broken heart or an empty stomach, rocksteady lyricists pleaded for the invisible spirit of the "Lord" to ease earthly pain and suffering. In the Wailers' "Somewhere to Lay My Head," Bob Marley pleaded for God to allow him an opportunity to rest from the burden of poverty and oppression (*One Love*). At other times, the singers praised God's inspirational and mysterious touch. In another Wailers' song, "I'm Gonna Put It On," optimism prevailed, as God's spirit inspired a "toast" to the "Lord" because he had stopped the "crying" (*One Love*). God was often called upon to assist the needy and cure the ill, but he had not yet materialized as an active force for universal justice.

God's relatively passive representation was balanced, however, by the Rude Boy, and the emerging Rastafarian theme that the oppressed must reclaim their own country. The Wailers, in particular, suggested in such songs as "Jailhouse," "Rude Boy," and "Freedom Time" that the Rude Boy would someday "rule" Jamaica, "walking" the "proud" land (*One Love*). Ken Boothe's song, "The Train Is Coming," vaguely encouraged Jamaicans to seek liberation in "this land [Jamaica] / Where we will all be free" (*Tougher Than Tough*). Rocksteady musicians had not articulated how the poor would reclaim Jamaica, and the music offered no concrete political or social strategies for salvation from the shantytown. The Rude Boy's instincts for the knife and gun, however, represented the turn from passively waiting for deliverance to a more active resistance against the police, the legal system, and the Jamaican government.

Rocksteady's vision of the future, however, still reflected the Rastafarian philosophy of peace and unity. Despite celebrating the Rude Boys' racial pride and violence, rocksteady songs envisioned a day when all Jamaicans would come together, and as U-Roy's "Everybody Bawling" put it, "live as one." The Wailers' "One Love" likewise preached unity in a memorable chorus that became something of a Rastafarian anthem: "One love / One heart / Let's get together / And feel all right" (*One Love*). The themes of unification and peace represented the Rastafarian response to bloodshed and dehumanization.

Rastafarian influences upon rocksteady were perhaps most clearly evident in the music's allusions to repatriation. In the song "This Train," the Wailers sang about being "saved," with the "holy" boarding a train bound for "glory" (*One Love*). Bob Andy's song, "I've Got to Go Back Home," envisioned an escape from the poverty and starvation in West Kingston with the repeated request to leave "this land" to "go back home" (*Tougher Than Tough*). Rocksteady musicians did not specifically link deliverance to the African continent. However, since over 90 percent of all Jamaicans were descendants of African slaves, many undoubtedly understood going "home" to mean repatriation to Africa. Although the Rastafarians' themes of peace and repatriation pervaded rocksteady, the music's sound became increasingly slower, sadder and, consequently, more politically meaningful.

Musical Instrumentation

As rocksteady emerged as Jamaica's new genre of popular music, a number of producers tried to take credit for this new musical development. Without a doubt, Duke Reid became synonymous with the rocksteady sound because, according to reggae expert Steve Barrow, he "was the producer who capitalised on this musical advance, who did more than anyone to define the sound" (15). Although the rocksteady sound was still marred by an uneven production quality, the introduction of four-track recording during the early to mid-1960s helped producers like Reid achieve a better sound quality.

It was during this period that rocksteady producers created a production technique called "versioning," a more expedient and less expensive method to produce records. Versioning is a process in which a new song is created by "taking the rhythm track of an old hit and have a singer 'voice' a new song on top of it" (Friedland 5). Reggae guitarist Ray Hitchins clarified the versioning process:

> Imagine Quincy Jones, for instance, taking the riddim [rhythm] track
> from Michael Jackson's hit song, "Beat It," and then asking Tina Turner to
> sing "What's Love Got to Do with It" over the same riddim. As you can
> imagine, Tina would say he's crazy (and perhaps you're thinking the same
> thing!), but this is precisely how reggae musicians have been forced to think
> and work—independent of the mainstream, with a method created by their
> own environment. (7)

Despite the development of new recording techniques, the new rocksteady arrangements continued to exhibit many of the same instrumental
qualities as its predecessor. Playing in the traditional offbeat rhythm, the
rhythm guitarist employed two or three major chords to create a "bright"
sound and followed a common chord progression (I, IV, V) borrowed from
R&B. While ska and rocksteady shared similar instrumental qualities, the
latter employed fewer horn instruments and highlighted the bass guitar and
the harmony vocals in slower, more soulful rhythms.

As suggested, a noticeable change in the tempo defined the rocksteady
era. Rocksteady often has been described as ska at half-speed (Steffens,
"Reggae" 883). While this is not technically accurate, rocksteady's dramatic change from the exhilarating tempo of ska to a slower, more soulful
pace signified a more serious, doubting music. While most ska songs
clipped along at 110–130 beats per minute (bpm), rocksteady songs, such
as Ken Boothe's "The Train Is Coming" (100 bpm), Alton and the Flames'
"Cry Tough" (96 bpm), Derrick Morgan's "Tougher Than Tough" (95
bpm), the Techniques' "Queen Majesty" (85 bpm) (*Tougher Than Tough*),
and the Jamaicans' "Ba Ba Boom" (76 bpm) (*Tougher Than Tough*), had a
noticeably slower tempo. It was as if the rocksteady rhythm invited the listener to slow down, to observe more closely the conditions in the shantytown, and to contemplate more deeply the need for change. The rhythmic
change and the use of fewer instruments allowed the previously submerged
vocals to move to the forefront.

Similar to ska, rocksteady featured offbeat musical figures. In many
songs, such as the Wailers' "Let Him Go" and Ken Boothe's "The Train
Is Coming," the guitar and piano would emphasize the characteristic

41

offbeat rhythmic pattern. However, rocksteady musicians began to integrate a two-guitar attack. In most cases, guitar #2 would simply double
rhythm guitar #1, producing a "fatter" and "fuller" sound. However, in
Alton Ellis's "Girl I've Got a Date" (*Tougher Than Tough*), guitar #2
strayed from its accompanying role and played a repetitive, muted, sin-
gle-note, fragmented riff. In this case, the role of the second guitarist
was to double the bass guitar pattern in order to ensure "that the [bass]
line would be heard no matter how bad the recording or listening envi-
ronment" (Bassford 45). This twin-guitar attack was perfected during
the early reggae period.

With increasing frequency, rocksteady musicians turned to the bass guitar to augment their musical statement. The electric bass guitar in rocksteady (typically not used in ska) "boomed" like a cannon. As rocksteady
musicians sang mournful words, the bass guitarist explored the low-end
potential of the instrument to establish a "fat" complementary tone. Rather
than playing a walking bass line, many rocksteady bassists often played a
repetitive pattern of short, quick notes intermingled with brief periods of
silence or rests. The song "Queen Majesty," recorded by the Techniques in
1967, exemplified this new approach (figure 2.1):

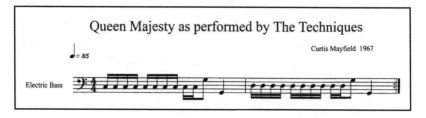

As the diagrams suggest, the bassist now played an active sixteenth-note
pattern rather than the walking bass line that emphasized the "one-note-
per-beat" quarter note style. During the first half of the bass line, the bassist
played four notes per beat; however, during the second half, the bassist left
"space" by resting on notes 12, 14, 15, and 16. In other words, dividing the
measure into 16 equal parts, the bassist played 12 out of 16 notes, leaving

space on notes 12, 14, 15, and 16. A simplified version of this bass rhythm would look like this (figure 2.2):

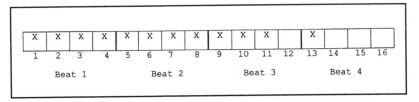

Jamaican bassist Jackie Jackson, who played on "Queen Majesty," described this new rocksteady bass sound:

> I was probably the first person to double up on a bass. . . . I can remember the first time I tried doubling up was on "Queen Majesty" by the Techniques. And it was hell inside that studio. Everybody said, "No, bass can't play so many notes. Bass so fast—it can't play so." And I say, "No, mon. Me play this today!" And that was how rocksteady was born. (qtd. in Gorney 41)

Jackson was also influential in the development of the Jamaican "riddim." Riddim is Jamaican slang for "rhythm." Bassists were responsible for developing a number of riddims, or signature repetitive bass lines, and a single riddim would be "the foundation on which numerous songs [30–40] could be recorded and released" (Hitchins 7). One rocksteady group, the Jamaicans, lyrically described the thunderous effect of this rocksteady rhythmic pattern as "Ba Ba Boom": "Everybody get ready / It's time to rocksteady / It's Ba Ba Boom time."

The rocksteady drummer continued to play a timekeeping role, emphasizing beats 2 and 4 on the snare drum while playing an eighth-note figure on the hi-hat or ride cymbal.[1] Similar to ska, some rocksteady songs featured a more adventurous percussion section. In Justin Hines and the Dominoes' "No Good Rudie" (*Duke Reid's*) the drummer would integrate drum rolls or other percussive techniques, influenced by both traditional Cuban music and calypso, to add color and "drive" to the rocksteady sound. And in the Wailers' "Let Him Go," the drummer was accompanied by several percussion instruments, including shakers, a guiro, and other instruments often used in Latin music.

The emphasis on the vocal group signaled a transition from the primarily instrumental form of ska to a vocal-oriented one with more of an emphasis on protest lyrics. Vocal techniques such as "rapping" (Bob Andy's "I've Got to Go Back Home"), call and response (the Wailers' "Jailhouse"), and vocal echo ("Cry Tough") increasingly became a part of the rocksteady sound.[2] In most cases, the lead vocal would plead, purr, suggest, and cry while the two harmony voices would function more like musical instruments, by humming, echoing, and complementing the lead vocal. In "Cry to Me," Bob Marley's lead vocal would be accompanied by the backing falsetto vocals of Peter Tosh and Bunny Wailer (*One Love*). Throughout the song, the vocals would sometimes merge into a unison line, while at other times the backing vocals would both repeat the lead chorus and respond with an answer. In rocksteady, the voice—as the most expressive and versatile musical "instrument"—was emphasized to an unprecedented degree, each voice in the ensemble interlocked in a harmony of protest.

In some ways, rocksteady closely mirrored ska's musical structure. By emphasizing the distinctive offbeat sound, rocksteady musicians stressed structured repetition and improvisation. However, in rocksteady, Jamaican musicians tried to develop a distinctive sound or musical style. Rocksteady employed few horns, introduced the bass guitar as the dominant instrument, and highlighted the vocal group to an unprecedented degree. With the advent of rocksteady, both the musical form and the lyrical content suggested a more politically active stance.

No longer willing to wait passively for repatriation, some Rastafarians were now actively demanding "liberation" in Jamaica. Over the next two decades, Rastafarian imagery increasingly would pervade Jamaica's popular music, and the demand for liberation of all Jamaicans from poverty and oppression would become louder and more insistent.

Chapter Three

EARLY REGGAE, BLACK POWER, AND THE POLITICIZATION OF RASTAFARI

The *sounds* of reggae . . . are the sounds of screeching tyres, bottles breaking, wailing sirens, gunfire, people screaming and shouting, children crying.
They are the sounds of the apocalyptic thunder and earthquake; of chaos and
curfews. The sounds of reggae are the sounds of a society in the process of
transformation, a society undergoing profound political and historical change.

—Linton Kwesi Johnson

As a young independent nation, Jamaica was growing up fast. The optimistic cry of "Forward March" heard following independence was replaced
with the panicked cry of the Ethiopians' 1968 song, "Everything Crash."
After the Jamaica Labour Party (JLP) retained political power in the 1967
elections, many Jamaicans feared a deepening economic crisis and five more
years of ruthless, autocratic leadership. As the JLP increased Jamaica's economic dependence on foreign countries and unemployment skyrocketed,
Rastafarians, radical academics, and the militant poor became a more unified

force of resistance. Many of these protest groups funneled their despair through the short-lived, but explosive, Black Power movement. The advent of the Black Power movement in Jamaica coincided with the publication of several Black Power newspapers, national strikes, violent demonstrations, and labor disputes.

The birth of reggae in 1968 signaled the beginning of a wholesale embrace of the Rastafarian faith and more radical political themes in Jamaican popular music. A whole generation began to wear dreadlocks, a Rastafarian hairstyle where the hair is neither cut nor combed, and to talk about Ethiopia and Mount Zion. While reggae musicians were influenced by both American R&B and soul music, many of these musicians started to make a musical exodus to Africa. Reggae's slower, heavier, almost hypnotic rhythms harkened a return to Africa. Reggae was also distinguished by the increased use of Jamaican patois, a language that combined both Standard English and African languages. More important, however, reggae became lyrically a more explicit medium of political protest.

While reggae revealed its political edge, the Rastafarian movement continued to struggle with the question of repatriation. The traditional Rastafarian tendency toward political withdrawal and spiritual meditation was challenged by calls to fight for human rights in Jamaica. During this period, some Rastafarians supported Jamaica's Black Power movement, especially the work of Walter Rodney, a University of the West Indies (UWI) professor and a spokesperson for the Black Power movement. At the same time, the Rastafarian Movement Association (RMA) established the movement's first newspaper, the *Rasta Voice*. The Rastafarians' new demands for liberation in Jamaica reflected a significant turn in the movement, receiving its clearest expression in the increasingly radical politics of Jamaican popular music.

While rocksteady gave expression to the vague Rastafarian promises of repatriation and unification, reggae musicians sang specifically about the Rastafarian concepts of "Jah," "Babylon," and "Mount Zion," and they openly promoted the spiritual pleasures of marijuana. They also developed historical narratives reminding the Jamaican people about the horrors of slavery, while ironically also promoting traditional Rastafarian themes of peace and

46

unification. Most important, however, reggae artists created a new, more aggressive image of the Rastafarian. Rocksteady's rebel, the Rude Boy, was the archetype for reggae's new outlaw, the Rastafarian "warrior." As depicted in reggae songs, Rastafarians were "beating," "whipping," and "conquering" the enemy "Babylon." The once-silent God became the Rastafarian deity, Jah, who "burned" his enemy in fire, as reggae advocated more aggressive political action in Jamaica as a prelude to repatriation to Africa.

JAMAICA: BLACK POWER AND THE WALTER RODNEY INCIDENT

By 1968, the JLP apparently had come to believe that radical factions and "foreign" influences were conspiring to undermine Jamaica's racial unity and political stability. The Rastafarian challenge became energized politically by the U.S. Black Power movement. The *Daily Gleaner* expressed the government's paranoia by splashing sensational headlines about student marches in France on the front page, along with pictures of U.S. cities engulfed in fire. Threatened by the rising tide of discontent and surprised by increasing agitation at the traditionally conservative University of the West Indies, the government implemented more repressive measures such as imprisonment and deportation in the name of law and order.

While the JLP may have been surprised by the emerging radicalism at UWI, the rise of protest against Jamaica's economic conditions could have been predicted. After independence, the JLP's "Five Year Plan" did not produce economic prosperity but, instead, even greater inequity of living conditions.[1] As the JLP encouraged foreign countries to invest in and expand Jamaica's manufacturing and bauxite industries, the traditional pursuits of agriculture, forestry, and fishing dropped to a low of 10 percent of Jamaica's gross domestic product in 1968 (Kuper 17). Consequently, Jamaica witnessed an increase in food imports. Food imports skyrocketed from J$45.9 million in 1969 to J$71.3 million in 1972 (Kuper 19).[2] The more Jamaica was forced to import food products, the higher the prices were on those goods. Perhaps the most devastating statistic, however, was the unemployment figure.

47

Unemployment figures rose from 13.5 percent in 1960 (Boyd 8–9) to 22.5 percent by October of 1972 (*Economic Survey of Jamaica 1972* 61).

Although increasingly tied to the U.S. economy, the Jamaican government clearly disapproved of one import from the mainland: radical black nationalism. Jamaican radicals had long admired U.S. Black Power advocates. Many Jamaicans had spent time in the United States visiting relatives or seeking job opportunities; some came back with "personal accounts" of the Black Power "challenge to U.S. racism" (Gray 150). In addition, some American Black Power leaders, most notably Stokely Carmichael, had been born and raised in the Caribbean. A radical black nationalist newspaper in Jamaica, *Abeng,* published stories on the U.S. Black Power movement, praising such supposedly violent radicals as Eldridge Cleaver and Stokley Carmichael ("Stokely" 1; "Forms of Violence" 4).

Within Jamaica itself, the chief voice of Black Power was Walter Rodney, a young Guyanese scholar of African history. Rodney, who attended UWI as an undergraduate from 1960 to 1963, received his doctorate in African history at the University of London in England. He later taught African history in Tanzania, Africa. In January 1968, Rodney returned to UWI as a visiting professor of African history, espousing what the JLP considered "subversive" views (Gray 161). Emphasizing the relationship between European imperialism and Jamaica's "petty-bourgeoisie" leadership, Rodney argued for blacks to fight against the injustices of Jamaican society (*Groundings* 27–8). After Marcus Garvey, Rodney was the first "West Indian to articulate in any coherent manner the philosophy of Black Power" (Gonsalves 2).

What set Rodney apart from most university activists was his efforts to teach African history in the impoverished areas of West Kingston. Published in 1969, Rodney's treatise on Black Power, *The Groundings with My Brothers,* described the relationship between Black Power and community activism: "I was prepared to go anywhere that any group of Black people were prepared to sit down to talk and listen. Because, that is Black Power, that is one of the elements, a sitting down together to reason, to 'ground' as the Brothers say" (63–4). Rodney also invited Rastafarians and other poor people to the UWI campus to attend his lectures. Rodney believed that the Rastafarian movement was an integral part of Jamaica's emerging black consciousness, because the movement rejected the "philistine white West Indian society" for the "cultural and spiritual roots in Ethiopia and Africa" (*Groundings* 61).

While other radical professors and some Rastafarians lauded Rodney's attempts to raise the consciousness of black Jamaicans, the JLP viewed Rodney as a serious threat to the stability of the country. On October 15, 1968, after returning from a Congress of Black Writers convention in Montreal, Canada, Rodney was declared *person non gratis* and was swiftly deported to Canada. The day after Rodney's deportation, UWI faculty and students protested the government's actions. What was planned as a "peaceful meeting" turned into a full-scale riot, leaving in its wake three dead, an estimated one hundred people arrested, fifty damaged buses, and property damages totaling over one million Jamaican dollars ("Diary of Events" 8; Gonsalves 9).

The government and the *Daily Gleaner* quickly put their own "spin" on the "Rodney Incident." Prime Minister Hugh Shearer expressed his disappointment with the UWI students who were involved with the demonstration: "I am disappointed that in their conferences and meetings they are still today discussing the lousy theory of Karl Marx which were [sic] enunciated in 1848, which is some 120 years ago" ("Text of Shearer's" 22). The prime minister concluded that there were "very substantial justifications" for deporting Rodney and warned the students that they have "been duped into supporting a destructive anti-Jamaican cause" ("Shearer Says" 7). Roy McNeill, minister of home affairs at Mona (a suburb of Kingston), believed the students had conspired against the government when they "contacted Rastafarian groups, known and dangerous criminals, political extremists and mal-contents" to supposedly recruit them for the demonstration. McNeill believed the protest was not a "peaceful demonstration" but an "incitement to violence" ("Students" 14).

The *Daily Gleaner* supported the government's decision to expel Rodney. In an editorial entitled "Cave Mona," the *Gleaner* pronounced that UWI "must not be allowed to be a cave for robbers of peace and plotters of disorder" (8). Columnist Tomas Wright speculated in his "Candidly Yours" column that the students have been "hypnotized" by a "tiny minority" (14). Apparently, the "Rodney Incident" established a pattern of thinking among many Jamaicans that Black Power was "evil" (Nettleford, *Identity* 117). Norman Girvan claimed that the JLP encouraged the riot because they knew it would later "associate the students and Rodney himself with a general image of arson, anarchy and riot" (61).

Five months after his deportation, Rodney continued to promote Jamaica's Black Power movement from abroad. In the March 1969 issue of the *Abeng*, Rodney pointed out that the "present government knows that Jamaica is a black man's country," and he argued that it "is afraid of the potential wrath of Jamaica's black and largely African population." Rodney urged a new Black Power movement in Jamaica that would break with imperialism, gain political power, and force the "cultural reconstruction of . . . the society in the image of the blacks" ("The Rise" 3).

Rodney was joined in his campaign by Marcus Garvey Jr., the son of the legendary Jamaican black nationalist leader. Also writing in *Abeng*, Garvey Jr. outlined the meaning of Black Power for Jamaicans: a pride in blackness, a knowledge of African history, and a reconstruction of black institutions and leadership. Garvey metaphorically explained the relevance of Black Power for Jamaicans: "[When] you have a huge black mass submerged in inferiority, like the hidden portion of an iceberg, it is obvious that Black Power is not only relevant but an absolute necessity for such people" ("Black Power" 3). As late as 1969, however, critics could still claim that Black Power had not attracted a "broad range of classes" in Jamaica, but was only "localized and confined to students, academics, workers, and a riotous group of unemployed protesters" (Gray 163). Even Garvey Jr. confessed that the movement had made little progress, lamenting that "it must be evident that 'Black Power' does not exist in Jamaica today" ("Black Power" 3).

Nevertheless, the ideology of Black Power became associated with the Rastafarian movement, and the Black Power ideology remained alive in the weekly newspaper, *Abeng*, which was first published in February 1969 and continued for ten months. In the first issue, the editors noted the connections between their Black Power philosophy and the community of oppressed Jamaicans coalesced by the increasingly political songs of Jamaica's popular musicians:

> We also share much in common with those Jamaican singers of today— singers whose statements about the society ring true. Their statements become electioneering slogans but are never examined for their true value. The most powerful medium, which has not been fully utilized, is the Sound System. . . . The *Abeng* in order to be meaningful realises that as a literary medium, it has to join forces with the rich oral tradition on which the Sound System is based. ("Abeng Sounds" 1)

Giving more political substance to the cause, *Abeng* also featured articles by UWI faculty members such as sociologist Trevor Munroe and economist George Beckford commenting on black nationalism and Jamaica's political parties. The paper also published a regular column by Ras Dizzy I., a Rastafarian journalist and poet, and the paper invited readers to contribute to a "Diary of Sufferers." The "Diary of Sufferers" featured Jamaicans describing their personal experiences of political victimization and police brutality. Although *Abeng* was not a Rastafarian publication, the newspaper sympathized with the Rastafarians, ultimately contributing to a wider schism between religiously apolitical Rastafarians and their more radical counterparts.

THE RASTAFARIAN MOVEMENT: RELIGION AND POLITICS

By the late 1960s, the Rastafarian movement had begun to attract the attention of students, radical academics, and some middle-class youths in Jamaica because of its association with Black Power. Marcus Garvey Jr. acknowledged the relationship between Rastafari and Black Power in Jamaica: "[Rastafari] held the torch of Africa alight at a trying time when the forces of evil had driven my father from the land. . . . It is they who now make it possible for me to emerge to a much easier task than I would have had if they had not existed" ("Marcus Garvey" 2). Although black leaders like Marcus Garvey Jr. and Walter Rodney were not members of the faith, they appreciated and identified with the Rastafarians' anti-colonial stance. As a longtime observer of Jamaica's social movements, Rex Nettleford, has noted, however, some Rastafarians were critical of the ideological tenets of Black Power: "Yet many of the older Rastafarians while sympathizing with the younger advocates' embrace of black nationalism questioned their sincerity on the key tenets of Repatriation and the divinity of Haile Selassie" (*Identity* 99).

At the end of the decade, the Rastafarian movement started publishing *Rasta Voice*, the movement's first official newspaper. *Rasta Voice* was the "official organ" of the Rastafarian Movement Association, one of the more "political" Rastafarian groups. Printed on ditto paper with cover drawings of Haile Selassie, the newspaper contained editorials, poems, short stories, and handwritten slogans, such as "Up with the Rasta-fari Movement" and "Free Ganga [sic] Now!"

The movement continued to reflect the tension between passively awaiting repatriation to Africa and political activism within Jamaica. In the *Rasta Voice*, and in the Black Power newspapers *Bongo-Man* and *Abeng*, some Rastafarians still argued for a return to Africa. In his article "Revolution or Repatriation?," Ras Dizzy I. suggested the incompatibility of the two goals, declaring that the "people must pledge their own determination for either government revolution or repatriation back to Africa." In the end, Dizzy argued for repatriation because it "is better to rest up in the desert with a hive of bees more than dwell with a den of fools" (4). In the December 1968 issue of *Bongo-Man*, Bongo Dizzy acknowledged that "we are truly humble people whose response to evil is to flee from it" (14). A writer with the pseudonym "Rasta Historian," writing in the *Bongo-Man*, agreed with Bongo Dizzy that "we have to go to Africa to live with our brothers and sisters there. Blacks remember, our King grant land space for us in Ethiopia [and] the world know [sic] it" (18).

Although the *Rasta Voice*, in particular, endorsed an eventual return to Africa, this did not blind the paper to the daily injustices in Jamaica. In an editorial entitled "A Poor Man's State in the Rich Men's Kindom [sic]," Ras

D. Bent complained that the "capitalist[s]" raised food prices so they "always have milk," but the poor "can't get it" (4). The editors of the *Rasta Voice* intimated that Rastafarians should observe these economic contradictions and "come together and slay the beasts of imperialism and capitalism" (Tucker 2).

The *Rasta Voice's* political agenda was also evident in its attacks on the University of the West Indies. Dubbing radical students at UWI phony "revolutionaries," the editors of the *Rasta Voice* claimed that they were "afraid of their own mothers and fathers." The real revolution, according to the editors, was not at the "U-Blind campus" but "out side [sic] where batons and gun-butts lick hard and dreadful. The cultural revolution, the African revolution, involves not books and talk and study groups, but personal reflection, meditation and scrutiny of self" (Rasta Voice Editorial Board 4).

In an editorial entitled, "U Blind Yu Can't See [sic]," I Ras I argued that

> True struggle cannot be defined by hierarchical relationships [sic] the student and the lecturer must become PEOPLE—AFRICAN PEOPLE before the[y] can claim to speak of LOVE, LIFE, DIGNITY, JUSTICE and FREEDOM. The student[s] shed their claims to superiority and humble themselves before JAH and MAN. They must come to RAS TAFARI because HE is the key to the[ir] own Regeneration and Revolution.(5)

Although the *Rasta Voice* did not publish articles on reggae music, the Rastafarian movement increasingly gave reggae its ideological content and musical direction. Rastafarian scholar Horace Campbell noted that the influence of Rastafari "on the development of the popular culture was evident by the fact that most serious reggae artists adhered to some of the principles of the Rastafarian movement" (*Rasta* 134). Although it is difficult to ascertain whether most Rastafarians actually identified with reggae, some scholars have noted that the Twelve Tribes of Israel, a "middle-class" Rastafarian group formed in 1968 under the leadership of Vernon Carrington, did embrace reggae as a new voice of Rastafari. In Jamaica, the often "privileged" brown class was designated "middle class" because members usually had the opportunity to attend college or to secure employment in the private sector. By popularizing the idea that reggae represented the movement, Twelve Tribes was also instrumental in providing "young whites [foreigners] with an accessible way of relating to Rasta" (Jones 170).

REGGAE: THE EARLY YEARS

Desmond Dekker's 1968 hit, "Israelites," portended the dramatic changes in Jamaica's popular music over the next decade (*King Kong*). The song, sung in a falsetto, referred obliquely to the Rastafarians as the "true" black Israelites, the lost Twelfth Tribe wandering in Babylon in search of their Ethiopian heaven, Mount Zion. The song, with its reference to "slaving" in Babylon "so that every mouth can be fed" illuminated the increasingly political message of the music, and the use of Jamaican patois demonstrated how reggae was becoming "darker and more African" (Hebdige, *Subculture* 37). Reggae's more African tones clearly marked a departure from rocksteady. Reggae "was clearly a Jamaican form of music which spoke directly to the social conditions of slavery"(Campbell, *Bob Marley* 7).

Many of Jamaica's leading rocksteady producers, such as Duke Reid, were disenchanted with reggae's increasing identification with the Rastafarian movement. The new early reggae producers, Edward "Bunny" Lee, Lee "Scratch" Perry, and Osborne Ruddock (known as King Tubby), however, supported reggae's new political leanings and had a major impact on the early direction of reggae. Tubby created "dub" music—instrumental reggae music mixed with some special effects (Barrow 14). While Tubby was creating dub music, Perry was instrumental in slowing down reggae's rhythms to allow the increasingly political messages to be heard (Barrow 19).

By 1968, reggae seemed at the brink of exploding onto the international music scene. Chris Blackwell, president of Island Records, created Trojan Records to market reggae music for international audiences. Reggae artist Jimmy Cliff released "Wonderful World, Beautiful People" in 1968, enjoying some international success. Bob Marley and the Wailers were also primed for international stardom. By the end of 1967, Marley signed a contract with JAD Records to write songs for Johnny Nash, the famous African American actor and musician. One product of this collaboration was Nash's reggae hit, "I Can See Clearly Now" (T. White 227–33).

Blackwell finally achieved major success in his efforts to popularize reggae internationally in the early 1970s. With the release in 1972 of the Wailers' first international record, *Catch a Fire*, and the international success in that same year of the movie and soundtrack, *The Harder They Come*, reggae suddenly seemed more than a passing musical novelty. Largely because of Blackwell's efforts to market reggae for international consumption, reggae became an international musical phenomenon.

Protest Lyrics

With rocksteady slowly retreating into the background, reggae musicians placed greater emphasis on protest themes. Early reggae placed more and more emphasis on the Rastafarian concepts of "Babylon," "Mount Zion," and "Jah." Reggae musicians identified Babylon as the European slave trader, the Jamaican government, or the police. Reggae artists also celebrated the Rastafarians' increasingly aggressive political protests and Jah's (Haile Selassie) powers as a vengeful God. In addition, reggae musicians sang about the spiritual pleasures of marijuana, used history as an ideological tool to educate Jamaican audiences about slavery, and combined calls for repatriation with protests against oppression in Jamaica.

While reggae songs continued the rocksteady tradition of expressing the personal pain of living in poverty, many reggae artists also began addressing more specific political and social issues. The Ethiopians' popular 1972 campaign song, "Everything Crash," recounted how Jamaica's social system had collapsed under the weight of national strikes in the 1960s (Waters 99). The Maytals' "54–46 (That's My Number)" critiqued Jamaica's penal system (*Tougher Than Tough*). Niney's "Blood & Fire" and the Wailers' "Fire Fire" employed the flame metaphor to comment on the struggle of the poor, deploring specifically the lack of water in the Kingston ghettos (*Tougher Than Tough*). Without water to cool the passions of the poor, the ghettos "burned" in revolution. Other reggae songs addressed more generally what

55

the Maytals called the "Pressure Drop." The pressure in the ghetto "dropped" when unemployment and homelessness exploded into gunshots and violence (*Harder They Come*).

In the early reggae period, the various enemies identified vaguely by rocksteady musicians—the police, the legal system—became fused into the distinctively Rastafarian enemy, "Babylon." Dennis Forsythe, in *Rastafari: For the Healing of the Nation*, has noted that the Rastafarian concept of Babylon was derived from "Babel"—the biblical city. In the Bible, the city of Babel symbolized a variety of evils: unmasked aggression toward its neighbors, moral degeneracy, and the worshiping of false deities (91). To underscore their own "captivity" in Jamaica, reggae musicians equated Babylon with the Roman Catholic church, the Jamaican government, the police, and various other political oppressors.

Many reggae musicians associated Babylon with particular people or institutions. The Melodians' "Rivers of Babylon," for example, took its inspiration from Psalms 137, and associated Babylon with European pirates and the African slave trade. The song provided a history lesson on Babylon's evils and encouraged the oppressed to call for "freedom." Under a loping rhythm, the lead voice remembered when the "wicked carried us away captivity," in a new "strange" land of plantations and forced labor (*Harder They Come*). Peter Tosh's "Dem [Them] Ha Fe [Have to] Get a Beatin" and Junior Byles's "Beat Down Babylon" equated Babylon with Jamaica's neo-colonialist government (Waters 134). Max Romeo identified Babylon with the corrupt and racist Jamaican police force:

> *I went to a party last Saturday night*
> *When I reached the party everything was all right*
> *Then Babylon raid, them raid, them raid . . .*
> *Batons sticks start flying, man start to bawl*
> *Some jump the fence, some put up defense*
> *But me catch me 'fraid, when Babylon raid.*
> *(qtd. in Waters 102–3)*

Reggae artists also used history as an ideological tool to address the question of slavery. The effort to teach "alternative" history lessons in songs can be attributed, at least in part, to the Rastafarians. Some Rastafarians have maintained that slavery never ended in Jamaica. In the Wailers' "400 Years," Peter Tosh's weary voice lamented "400 years" of the "same old philosophy" (*Collection Vol. 3*). The Abyssinians' "Declaration of Rights" narrated how "Africans" were removed from "civilization" to "slave in this big plantation" (*Satta Massagana*). As reggae matured in the 1970s, musicians believed it was important to provide the Jamaican people with an "alternative history" in a struggle to overcome "mental slavery."

The Rastafarian influence also could be heard in songs promoting the use of ganja or marijuana. Many Rastafarians smoked marijuana as a religious sacrament, believing that it helped them communicate with God. Jamaican folklore also held that marijuana had miraculous healing powers—the power to cure a variety of diseases. Four years before Peter Tosh's 1976 ganja anthem "Legalize It" was banned from the airwaves in Jamaica, the Wailers celebrated marijuana more subtlety in "African Herbsman" and "Kaya" (*History of Trojan*). Under the haze of the sweet smell of ganja, "Kaya" showcased the request "to have fire now," as Bob Marley celebrated the "good" pleasures of ganja. As the song drifted into a hypnotic pulse, Marley testified that the drug lifted him "so high" he could "touch the sky." In one of the most obvious attempts to promote the spiritual pleasures of ganja, Niney sang in "Blood & Fire": "Blessed is the pipe that is always light / In the house of Jah Rastafari / Blessed is the weed of the ganja seed / That keeps the breeding the ganja breed."

While Rastafarians testified to the spiritual powers of ganja, other musicians sang about the Rastafarian god, Jah. Haile Selassie, or Jah, became the living black god. In ska and rocksteady songs, God's role was that of a silent redeemer. In the early reggae phrase, Jah's role included both redeeming the faithful and punishing "Babylon." In Max Romeo's "Let the Power Fall on I," Jah "burn[ed]" the wicked to "ash" (qtd. in Waters 133). In "Lick It Back Jah," I-Roy challenged his enemy to "resist Jah." Jah had the power to "lick . . . back" the "bald head[s]," or non-Rastafarians (qtd. in Brodber and Greene 8).

Niney's "Blood & Fire" warned that in the "House of Jah Rastafari," judgment had "come" and mercy had "gone." In the Newcomers' "Killing Jamaica Children," Jah condemned Babylon for starving "Jah Jah children" (qtd. in L. Johnson, "The Politics" 364). With the advent of reggae, the silent, redeeming God of rocksteady increasingly became Jah, the vengeful God.

While the rocksteady period reflected the portrait of an aggressive Rude Boy, reggae musicians developed the imagery of a more aggressive Rastafarian "warrior." In "Beat Down Babylon," the "righteous Rastaman" advocated "whip[pings]" and "beat[ings]" to destroy "wicked men" (qtd. in Waters 132). In an early version of the Wailers' "Duppy Conqueror," the singer's desire to cross the bridge to Mount Zion was temporarily thwarted by a "bull-bucker," a Rastafarian term for "bully" (*Collection Vol. 3*). In order to complete the journey to Mount Zion, the singer promised that the "duppy," a Jamaican term for a dead spirit, would be "conquered." In "Dem Ha Fe Get a Beatin," Peter Tosh declared that the "wicked" had "reign[ed] too long" (qtd. in Waters 134). Rejecting the strategy of nonviolence, Tosh repeated the call to "beat" the "wicked." The Wailers' "Small Axe," while casting Babylon ambiguously as the "big tree," identified the Rastafarians as the "small axe ready to cut you down" (*Collection Vol. 3*). In contrast to the traditional Rastafarian philosophy of love and nonviolence, reggae songs had the Rastafarians "beating," "whipping," "cutting," and "conquering" the enemy.

Nevertheless, many reggae musicians continued to promote the themes of unification and peace. Ken Boothe declared that the "chains" of illiteracy and oppression would be lifted and people would "unite" on "freedom street" (*King Kong*). Other reggae songs, including Greyhound's song "Black and White," encouraged blacks and whites to live in "peace and love" (*History of Trojan*). Nicky Thomas's "Love of the Common People" challenged Jamaicans to "love" the dispossessed lower classes (*History of Trojan*). The Uniques' song "My Conversation" urged Jamaicans "to love your brothers and sisters" (*Tougher Than Tough*). Roman Stewart's "Live and Learn" reminded Jamaicans of the necessity of coexistence, while U-Roy's "Stick Together" pleaded for Jamaicans to "stick together" and "love one another" (*Masters of Reggae*).

Reggae musicians continued to promote repatriation as the ultimate solution to the problem of oppression. The Abyssinians believed that Rastafarians would "Forward unto Zion" (*Satta Massagana*); the Black Arks were instructing the oppressed to "get out of Babylon" (*Masters of Reggae*); and the Wailers located the Rastafarian heaven, "Holy Mount Zion," in Africa. In "400 Years," Peter Tosh concluded the song's dissonant tale with promises that the oppressed would eventually leave Jamaica for their own "land of liberty." In another Wailers' song, "Stop That Train," Peter Tosh employed a train metaphor to illustrate the promise of repatriation. Lamenting the division between wealth and poverty, and claiming that he could not "find happiness," Tosh repeatedly declared his commitment to repatriation in the chorus of the song: "Stop this train / I'm leaving" (*Collection Vol. 3*).

Musical Instrumentation

As a musical form, reggae echoed ska's jaunty, offbeat guitar and rocksteady's emphasis on the electric bass guitar and vocal harmony. The early reggae sound downplayed the horn section, however, and songs such as "400 Years" encouraged musicians to slow the reggae rhythm to match the hypnotic pulse of Rastafarian drumming. As producers Lee Perry and King Tubby were experimenting with the new reggae sound, the keyboards became more important components in the reggae ensemble. The organ assumed an important supportive role, providing a colorful, rich texture to the reggae arrangement.

Much like its predecessors, ska and rocksteady, early reggae producers would "audition" new reggae songs to dancehall crowds at night before committing only the most popular songs to vinyl (Friedland 5). Reggae expert Steve Barrow noted that reggae music—compared to American rock-and-roll—was still produced quickly and inexpensively: "Whereas a rock group might take a year to produce a concept album, Bunny Lee in Kingston could, and did, make three albums in one night" (19).

Although the production value of reggae music improved slightly with the introduction of multi-track recording, many early reggae songs were still recorded on basic recording equipment in Kingston. For this reason, early reggae music still suffered from a "primitive" and "unsophisticated" sound. In some cases, the instruments were out of tune, poorly miked, under-recorded, and crudely mixed. Yet, the production style also added to the authenticity of the music, emphasizing its immediate, raw, street-level sound. In time, some observers would distinguish between authentic Jamaican reggae music and its international counterpart.

Similar to ska, early reggae music evolved through two distinct phases. In the first phase (1968–1970), the transition from rocksteady to reggae, the reggae tempo increased slightly. Many songs during this period, including the Melodians' "Rivers of Babylon" (107 bpm), the Wailers' "African Herbsman" (109 bpm), Bob and Marcia's "Young Gifted & Black" (117 bpm), and Ken Boothe's "Freedom Street" (130 bpm), reflected quick, pulsating reggae rhythms. Despite the increased tempo, early reggae songs employed fewer instruments playing fewer notes, resulting in a less "dense," more sparse sound. Consequently, the new reggae arrangement contained more "rests" or "space" between the pulsating rhythmic patterns of the instruments. The second phase (beginning in 1971) was characterized by slower tempos and an overall "laid-back," more hypnotic sound.

Early reggae music continued to create aural space for the lead vocal and harmonies to advocate political and social change. Increasingly, however, the vocal lines became more intertwined and structurally complex. Reggae songs, for example, would often incorporate a number of vocal techniques. In the Maytals' song "54–46 (That's My Number)," the song opened with the lead singer, Fred (Toots) Hibbert, singing "I say 'ya'" in a joyous tone. In each instance, the two backup vocals "responded" to the lead vocal by repeating the phrase. After the introduction, Hibbert used a half-talking, half-singing approach to describe his arrest and imprisonment in a Jamaican jail. While describing his experiences, the backup vocalists shifted to a harmonic role, underpinning the narrative with a basic "ooh" harmony line. As the song slipped into the chorus, the singer and backup vocals sang in unison. This song clearly exemplified the diverse vocal roles performed during the early reggae period.

In a more dramatic example, the song "Rivers of Babylon" employed a very complex vocal delivery. During the first part of the song, the lead vocalist and the two background vocals sang in harmony:

> *By the Rivers of Babylon*
> *Where he sat down*
> *And there he went*
> *When he remembered Zion*
> *But the wicked carried us away captivity*
> *Require from us a song*
> *How can we sing King Alfa's song*
> *In a strange land*

In the next section of the song [1:16], the lead vocalist (now loosely double-tracked)[3] shifted from singing a structured, harmonized part to a freer, improvisational mode, echoed by harmony parts:

1. Lead vocal (Left channel [L]):   Sing it out loud

   (Right channel [R]): Sing it out loud

Harmony: ah-ah-ah-ah

2. Lead [L]:   Sing a song of freedom sister

   [R]:   Sing a song of freedom brother

Harmony: ah-ah-ah-ah

3. Lead [L]:   Sing a song of freedom bro-brother-her-her-her

   [R]:   Sing a song of freedom sis-sister-her

Harmony: ah-ah-ah-ah

4. Lead [L]:   whoa-oh-oh-oh oh-oh-oh na-na

   [R]:   na-na-na-na na-ah-ah na-na

Harmony: ah-ah-ah-ah

5. Lead vocal [L]:   hmm-hmm-hmm

        [R]:   hmm-hmm-hmm

In the first vocal phase, both the left and right vocal parts sang the same lyric, but with slightly different inflections. In the next phase, the lead vocals sang the identical lyrical phrase until the last word in that line. At this point, the left vocal shouted "sister," while the vocal part in the right channel yelled "brother." At the end of the third phrase, the left and right vocal parts not only traded the words "brother" and "sister," but each part improvised a slightly different vocal embellishment to conclude the phrase. In the fourth phrase, the left and right vocal parts sang near identical notes and rhythms, but employed different word syllables. As illustrated, with each successive phrase, the left and right vocal parts became increasingly creative and improvisational in nature.

Heavily influenced by R&B, soul, and the emerging funk sounds of James Brown, most reggae songs introduced a twin-guitar attack, with each guitar playing separate, but important rhythmic functions. Guitar #1 continued to play the typical offbeat figure (commonly called "bang" or "skank" in reggae lexicon) creating reggae's distinctive and unique sound, while also utilizing a clear and bright percussive sound and mid-ranged chord voicings.

Similar to American black music, guitar #1 would "chop out" a simple chord progression based on a familiar pattern of primary chords (I, IV, V). Most reggae songs contained two (e.g., "African Herbsman" [Bb and Gm]) or three chords (e.g., Eric Donaldson's "Cherry Oh Baby" [B, E, and F#]). In contrast, a few reggae songs such as the cover of the American recording, "Young Gifted & Black" [*Tougher Than Tough*], employed a fairly sophisticated chord structure containing seven chords as opposed to two or three. In addition to the primary or major chords (C [I], F [IV], and G [V]), the song also incorporated the three secondary or minor chords (Dm [ii], Em [iii], and Am [vi]). The use of the F/G chord and the addition of a string section lent a Broadway or showtune-like influence to the song. And unlike many reggae songs of this period, this song had a smooth and polished sound, allowing all of the instruments to be heard clearly in the mix.

Despite the similarities to rocksteady, the rhythm style of guitar #1 evolved during this period. Reggae guitarists started to "double up, playing sixteenth notes on the upbeat instead of the eighth note patterns of Rock Steady" (Friedland 7).

Assuming a different stylistic approach, guitar #2 played a repetitive, muted, fragmented riff, often in unison with the bass guitar. For example, in Desmond Dekker's song "Israelites" (figure 3.1), this unison riff acted as the musical "backbone" for most of the song:

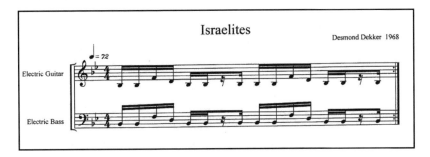

The second guitarist and the bassist were able to create a seamless musical "groove" by implementing consistent volume levels, similar muted tones, and near-exact doubling of notes and rhythms. In fact, the casual listener would most likely perceive the two sounds as emanating from one instrument.

The electric bass guitar played an increasingly important role in the reggae arrangement. Similar to rocksteady, the reggae bassist played a riddim based upon a repetitive pattern of notes followed by a brief pause or rest. To anchor the sound and provide a counter-statement to the often scratchy, trebly rhythm guitar, the bass guitarist utilized a full-bodied, deep, warm, fat, and round sound.

During this period, the bass guitarist employed a number of diverse rhythmic patterns. And while many reggae songs (e.g., the Ethiopians' "Reggae Hit the Town") featured a sixteenth-note pattern, in some songs, such as "54–46 (That's My Number)," the bass guitarist would occasionally play quarter and eighth notes interspersed within a sixteenth-note riddim pattern. Despite the fact that many reggae songs employed a sixteenth-note bass figure,

> Reggae bass playing is very laid back. You will see many examples that contain sixteenth-note rhythms, yet the articulation must be relaxed—almost lazy. The Reggae sixteenth note is not the same as a Fusion sixteenth note. The groove is very heavy and the downbeat must be played with conviction. (Friedland 9)

While the bass guitarist was experimenting with new riddim patterns, the drummer continued to perform the traditional timekeeping role, occasionally employing snare fills and busier improvisational percussion work. For the most part, however, the drums still served to provide reggae with a steady, hypnotic "groove" primarily based on repetition. The constant, unyielding drum beat helped turn the reggae song into a musical form without a beginning, middle, or end.

However, the drums—especially during the first phase of the early reggae period—were often underrecorded, and in some cases, almost inaudible. For example, in the songs "Israelites" and "Reggae Hit the Town" the drums were often mixed so low that only the snare and the hi-hat were audible to the listener. In the song "Blood & Fire" the bass drum was seemingly the only audible component of the drum kit. By the mid-1970s, however, the partnership of drummer Sly Dunbar and bassist Robbie Shakespeare would refine and redefine reggae's rhythm section. In addition, advancements in recording techniques allowed the bass and drums to be moved to the front of the audio mix, thus solidifying the contemporary reggae sound.

The early reggae arrangements also showcased the multiple roles of the electronic organ. In songs such as the Harry J. Allstars' "The Liquidator" and Lloydie and the Lowbites' sexually outrageous "Birth Control," the organist played an independent, yet supportive, riff which added richness to the reggae arrangement (*History of Trojan*). In other songs, the organist would simply provide a chordal accompaniment to the guitar and the drums. For example, in the song "Cherry Oh Baby," the organist doubled rhythm guitar #1, reinforcing the song's harmonic structure. In many reggae songs, the role of the organist was to "connect" with the bass guitar and bass drum and communicate a warm, pleasant-sounding backdrop (Ehrlich 54). Finally, the organist would occasionally act as a counterpart to rhythm guitar #1. In "Rivers of Babylon" the organist "filled space" by playing on the downbeat while the rhythm guitar emphasized the upbeat.

In total, the early reggae arrangement was characterized by both repetition and improvisation. The bass guitar and drums provided the repetitive riddim figure; guitar #1 played a chordal figure; and guitar #2 would usually double the bass guitar. The reggae arrangement, of course, did not normally include instrumental solos that were present in reggae's influences, including R&B and soul music. The noted exception to this rule was the occasional liberties taken by the lead vocalists and the horns.

As the Rastafarian movement continued to reveal its increased political consciousness in popular music, Jamaican authorities responded with strategies to "control" the movement. The *Gleaner* vilified the movement as a threat to national security, and the police disrupted Rastafarian meetings and imprisoned members. The broadcast media restricted the exposure of Jamaica's protest music, and during a national crisis, the JLP even placed a broadcast ban on "anti-JLP" songs. The next chapter explores in greater depth these efforts to control the Rastafarian movement.

Chapter Four

THE JAMAICA
LABOUR PARTY'S
"POLICY OF THE BEAST"

The Rhetoric of Social Control Strategies

And whilst these body-blows are coming in they're kissing your cheeks with Trips to Africa and Hints of Possible Links with Ethiopia . . . we've watched the policy of the Beast shifting from outright brutality and duplicity to the more subtle approach of a few surface concessions.

—A. King

Since the 1930s, the Rastafarian movement has been in conflict with Jamaica's colonialist web of economic exploitation and racial stratification. While the Rastafarian religion traditionally has emphasized repatriation back to Africa, the movement also has agitated for a number of political reforms in Jamaica. This politicization of Rastafari may be traced to Haile Selassie's 1966 dictum, "liberation before repatriation," yet the Jamaican government perceived the movement as a threat long before Selassie's visit

66

to Jamaica. Determined to maintain a neo-colonial social structure even after independence, and committed to a capitalist economic program dependent on political stability, Jamaica's ruling class had long viewed Rastafari as a threat, if not in physical terms, then at least symbolically. As symbols of racial injustice and poverty in Jamaica, the simple visibility of Rastafarians—a visibility increased dramatically by the popularity of reggae music—challenged the legitimacy and power of Jamaica's ruling elite.

The Jamaican government and its surrogates employed a number of different strategies simultaneously to control the movement, apparently depending on the nature of the challenge being posed. In response to Rastafarian demands for repatriation and other essentially nonthreatening demands, the Jamaican government generally employed relatively moderate strategies of social control, such as "evasion" and "counter-persuasion." In Jamaica, the government's strategy of "evasion" included two major tactics: "investigations" of its demands for repatriation, and denial of access to the public airwaves. At the same time, the government employed the "counter-persuasion" strategy. This strategy challenges a "social movement's version of reality and [seeks] to discredit leaders, members, and demands" (Stewart, Smith, and Denton 150). This the Jamaican government did both by creating a myth of "Jamaican Exceptionalism," which denied movement claims about racial and class divisions in Jamaica, and through the tactics of ridicule and fear appeals of a Rastafarian uprising in Jamaica.

The government also used the most repressive strategy of social control: "coercion." Typically targeted at a movement's leadership, coercion may involve tactics ranging from "coercive persuasion," such as threats and general harassment, to more physical tactics, including imprisonment or banishment. Failing to stem Rastafarian agitation in Jamaica, the government turned to the strategy of "adjustment." This strategy includes the tactics of incorporating the personnel of the agitation movement into the mainstream political system and accepting some of the means of agitation. Despite these efforts to control the Rastafarian movement and reggae music, the movement continued to gain popularity and some political influence in the 1960s.

THE JAMAICAN GOVERNMENT AND THE DOMINANT CLASSES

The Jamaican government's efforts at social control between 1959 and 1971 must be viewed in the context of that nation's history of European colonialism and social stratification based on race and class. In order to maintain the institution of slavery in Jamaica, Jamaica's colonial ruler, Great Britain, sought to destroy the slaves' African identity. Toward this end, European colonialists employed a variety of tactics, including the distortion of African history, colonial education, the promotion of self-hatred, and dehumanization. According to Jamaican anthropologist Barry Chevannes, European colonialists defined Africa as the "dark" and "silent" continent, and blackness was personified as "Satanic," "uncivilized," "savage," "backward," and "immoral." Descended from heaven, Europe presumably was materialized in purity, innocence, and beauty ("Race" 139).

In order to perpetuate European hegemony, the British colonial powers also sustained a rigid social stratification in Jamaica. In Jamaica, there historically has been an asymmetrical relationship between the powerful white minority and powerless black majority. By the end of the eighteenth century, the white planter class of eighteen thousand settlers ruled over a quarter of a million slaves (Broom 115). Since then, the number of whites on the island has decreased steadily. By the late 1990s, whites comprised approximately 3 percent of the Jamaican population, but they along with the brown middle class continued to control the politics and economy of the island.

Jamaica's white planter class has maintained its political power largely through the support of a brown or mulatto Jamaican middle class. Historically, the middle class in Jamaica was a product of interracial sexual contact between white planters and black slaves. As in American slavery, the white foreign slave owner viewed the African woman as property, and rape was commonplace on the plantation. The children of these concubines were often given special treatment and privileges. Some were sent to schools in Europe. Some were placed in government jobs. The white planter class still treated the mulatto class as "second-class citizens," but they encouraged them to emulate European values and rewarded those who did. Since the formation of Jamaica's political parties during the early 1940s, the brown middle class has generally held the balance of political power in Jamaica. As Rex Nettleford noted, "As the pure white population dwindled, the free coloureds became the heirs to the European position and power and regarded themselves as the rightful sons of the Jamaican soil" (*Identity* 28–9).

After the fall of colonial rule in 1962, Jamaica's political parties, the JLP and the PNP, maintained the British social and political structure, and the result was a type of neo-colonialism, not genuine independence. Like the British rulers who came before them, the new ruling class in Jamaica encouraged its citizens, especially the middle class, to embrace white European values and emulate British culture. Unfortunately for the ruling class, this neo-colonialism became increasingly difficult to maintain in the mid- to late 1960s, as the anti-colonial and Black Power impulses sweeping the world were manifested in Jamaica in a more politically challenging Rastafarian movement.

STRATEGY OF EVASION

Responding to the agitation of a social movement, "establishments" tend to resort first to the strategy of "evasion," which involves, in effect, pretending "that it does not exist or that it is too insignificant to recognize" (Stewart, Smith, and Denton 149). The strategy of evasion can involve several tactics designed to render the movement "'invisible'" or to "slow or delay the decision-making process regarding a social movement's charges and demands" (Stewart, Smith, and Denton 149–50). Establishments can postpone action, appear constrained to grant protest goals (Lipsky 1156), control or change the social and political agenda (Simons, *Persuasion* 275–6), purchase more "media time and space" than social movement leaders (Simons, Mechling, and Schreier 831–2), and divert movement demands into bureaucratic channels by establishing committees, commissions, or task forces to "investigate" movement concerns (Stewart, Smith, and Denton 150). Those in power may even simply refuse to meet with social movement leaders.

In responding to a social movement employing music as its primary mode of communication, however, one tactic of "evasion" is especially attractive: the "denial of means." As Bowers, Ochs, and Jensen explain, "denial of means" involves denying protestors the "physical means"—meeting places, printing presses, sound equipment, and the like—to "effectively promulgate their ideas and demands" (52).

During the 1960s, the most obvious form of "evasion" employed by the Jamaican government was the effort to divert Rastafarian demands for repatriation into bureaucratic channels. Based on a recommendation from the 1960 pamphlet, the *Report on the Rastafari Movement in Kingston, Jamaica*—a report derived from an intensive two-week study by three researchers from the University of the West Indies (UWI)—PNP Prime Minister Norman Manley sent a nine-member delegation to Africa in 1961 to investigate the feasibility of the movement's demands for repatriation. In the process, however, Manley and the PNP government reclassified the demand for "repatriation" as simply one issue in Jamaica's wider debate over emigration policies. According to Nettleford,

> The idea of repatriation was seen to be antagonistic to the nationalism of the status quo though the notion of migrating is not deemed incompatible. The "dropping-out" of the society is regarded as a betrayal of the ideals of Jamaican unity in diversity, and assertive language for change is seen as a major threat to the proverbial "stability of the country." (*Identity* 59)

By reclassifying the Rastafarian demand for "repatriation" as merely an issue of "migration," Manley could justify the Back-to-Africa mission as a part of Jamaica's long-standing policy of assisting "surplus" Jamaicans who sought to emigrate to the United States or Britain (Nettleford, *Identity* 68). According to Nettleford, Manley treated Africa as simply "a new outlet for Jamaica's surplus population" (*Identity* 70). More important, the Rastafarians were represented as only one group seeking migration to Africa. As the negotiations dragged on over the next two years, the initial Rastafarian cry for repatriation was increasingly muffled within this larger discussion of emigration.

The Mission to Africa, as the committee was called, traveled to five African nations—Ethiopia, Nigeria, Liberia, Ghana, and Sierra Leone—and met with government officials to discuss the idea of Jamaican blacks emigrating and gaining citizenship in Africa. The delegation included Jamaican representatives from the Universal Negro Improvement Association (UNIA), the Afro-Caribbean League (ACL), the Ethiopian World Federation (EWF), the Afro-West Indian Welfare League (AIWL), and three self-appointed spokespersons from the Rastafarian movement. The committee published its findings in the 1961 pamphlet, *Majority Report of Mission to Africa*. According to the pamphlet, many of the African officials were prepared to accept the repatriation of "Africans living abroad" (1). Despite this initial acceptance, however, African government officials were concerned, according to the report, that Jamaicans exposed to "western ideals and customs" would find it difficult to assimilate to African culture (2). Furthermore, as the report suggested, African countries desired emigrants who possessed "artisan" skills, such as mechanics or carpenters (1).

After the committee had published its report, the Jamaican government made no formal plan to assist Jamaicans wanting to emigrate to Africa. According to Nettleford, Manley instead established a second committee, called the "Working Party," to further investigate the Rastafarian demands (*Identity* 69). The Working Party recommended yet another mission to Africa, and in January 1962, the Jamaican government sent what it called a "Technical Mission" to Ethiopia, Nigeria, and Ghana (Nettleford, *Identity* 70). During the talks between R. A. Foreman, former chairperson of the Working Party, and representatives from the three African countries, the Technical Mission learned that Ghana and Nigeria were still only interested in admitting skilled or professional Jamaicans (Nettleford, *Identity* 70). Most Rastafarians simply did not have the skills to meet such requirements. The Ethiopian government, however, agreed to accept Jamaican farmers and to provide them with land (Nettleford, *Identity* 70).

In the spring of 1962, the Technical Mission submitted specific proposals to Ethiopia for allowing Jamaicans to settle in Ethiopia. The plan to send Jamaicans to Ethiopia, however, never materialized. While the

Ethiopia Court was debating Jamaica's proposal, Manley lost the 1962 national election and the new JLP government "plunged into preparations for Independence." As a result, the JLP government "shelved" the issue of repatriation for "the rest of the decade" (Nettleford, *Identity* 70–1). The PNP had "evaded" the demand for repatriation, and just as it appeared that real progress had been made, the JLP simply killed the plan. In the final analysis, however, the whole episode only increased the sense among some Rastafarians that repatriation was indeed a realistic possibility.

A second evasion tactic, denial of means, likewise failed ultimately to control the agitation of the Rastafarian movement. Potentially an effective weapon against a movement dependent on music as means of protest, denial of means involved denying a movement the media or forums to spread its ideas. In Jamaica, this involved simply censoring or even banning popular protest music. In the view of Jamaica's dominant classes, any cultural arti- fact considered "African" posed a threat to the established order. Under colonial rule, Jamaica's dominant classes were indoctrinated with the belief that "high-brow" foreign music was "superior" to the "primitive" music of home. According to Dermot Hussey, the upper classes had been condi- tioned "to look outside to a music being a better music." This conditioning underlay efforts to keep indigenous music—and especially politically threat- ening indigenous music—off of Jamaica's public airwaves.

Two companies historically have controlled the broadcast media in Jamaica. In 1950, Jamaica's first mainstream radio station, Radio Jamaica Re- diffusion Limited (RJR) was established as an independent, privately owned subsidiary of a Great Britain telecommunications corporation, Rediffusion of London (A. Brown, "Mass Media" 19). The station reflected the interests of its British owners with "no particular commitment to national cultural expres- sion" (A. Brown, "Mass Media" 19). During the 1950s, the station's playlist was dominated heavily by American and British popular and classical music. Jamaican popular music received very limited airplay (Witmer 13).

In 1959, PNP Prime Minister Norman Manley facilitated the creation of Jamaica's second mainstream radio station, the Jamaica Broadcasting Corpo- ration. Supposedly, the JBC was created as a "vehicle for Jamaican creative cultural expression." Unlike the RJR, the JBC was government controlled and managed by a "government-appointed Board of Directors with a General Manager as [its] chief executive" (A. Brown, "Mass Media" 18). According to Hussey, shortly after the creation of the JBC, ska musician Theophilus Beckford recorded his rollicking hit, "Easy Snappin'," in a JBC studio.

Yet even the JBC continued to favor foreign music over Jamaica's indigenous forms. More important, both stations, when they did play indigenous music, promoted ska musicians who played safe, nonpolitical songs. The lyrics of many of these songs reflected romantic themes, and the instrumentation was often "clean[ed] up" for the tastes of "white audiences abroad" (Hebdige, *Cut* 67). In one case, British musicians were hired to provide the lush instrumentation behind Millie Small's bubbly 1964 hit "My Boy Lollipop" (Jones 58). As sociologist Simon Jones has argued, however, these attempts to present "safe" groups like Byron Lee and the Dragonaires as "authentic" ska musicians did not fool many Jamaicans. The creative base for ska music "remained firmly rooted in the working-class ghettoes of Kingston throughout most of the 1960s" (22).

As ska evolved into the more politically threatening forms of rocksteady and reggae, the Jamaican government more actively denied the movement the "means of protest" by simply banning certain songs from the public airwaves. Dermot Hussey experienced first hand the government's method of censorship. A governmental official would, according to Hussey, contact the radio station's program manager and request—or often demand—that a song be removed from the playlist. In the year leading up to the 1972 national elections, the JLP banned several "PNP" campaign songs, including the Wailers' militant "Small Axe," Delroy Wilson's optimistic "Better Must Come," and the Abyssinians' "Declaration of Rights" (Waters 102). According to sociologist Anita Waters, who has studied the relationship between reggae and Jamaican politics, even indigenous music that was not banned received minimal airplay (102).

Yet Jamaica's lower classes had a way to circumvent the establishment's control over the public airwaves. With portable public address systems known as "sound systems," they had, in effect, their own radio station on wheels. Sound-system operators would drive their vans into neighborhood dances in Kingston and play ska or R&B music on high-fidelity playback equipment. Despite being banned from the radio stations, for example, the Wailers' "Small Axe" could be heard during the 1972 campaign, as Waters has reported, in "slum beer joints and on sound systems in the countryside and in urban dance halls" (102). The sound system proved an effective means of counteracting the restrictive policies of the radio stations and the government's practice of censorship. The attempt to deny Rastafarians and other lower-class Jamaicans access to "their" music only increased the demand for "sound systems" and for the songs that had been banned.

Failing to "evade" the challenge posed by the movement, the Jamaican government and its surrogates therefore also employed a second strategy of social control—the strategy of "counter-persuasion." This strategy, however, rarely worked.

THE STRATEGY OF COUNTER-PERSUASION

When "evasion" fails, those in power typically turn to a more active strategy of social control—the strategy of "counter-persuasion." In "counter-persuasion," governments and their surrogates seek to discredit movement leaders or to show that their ideas are "ill-advised and lacking merit"(Stewart, Smith, and Denton 150). Counter-persuasion may be part of a larger rhetorical matrix called "administrative rhetoric," or the establishment's attempt to undermine a social movement's ideas and influence (Windt 247). A number of counter-persuasion tactics have been identified, including ridicule, appealing to unity by "crying anarchy" (A. King, "The Rhetoric" 128–9), and linguistic control (Fanon 47).

In Jamaica, the strategy of counter-persuasion took two major forms: the creation of a myth of "Jamaican Exceptionalism," which countered movement portraits of a nation divided by race and class, and the use of ridicule and fear appeals to discredit the Rastafarian movement. By the end of the 1960s, however, the realities of life in Jamaica had destroyed the myth of Jamaican Exceptionalism, and the hysterical and contradictory portrait of the Rastafarians as "lazy revolutionaries" apparently did not "ring true" for most Jamaicans, especially the lower classes.

The government's most obvious tactic of counter-persuasion was a rhetoric of national unity, which characterized Jamaica as a utopian paradise of racial harmony. As Rex Nettleford has observed, the government tried to define Jamaica as a "non-racial" country where a "'mixture of races liv[ed] in perfect harmony'" (*Identity* 23). Political scientist Obika Gray calls this rhetoric "Jamaican Exceptionalism," which Gray described further in his book: "The appeal to the overwhelming black population was that they were a special people in the world, who lived harmoniously with other domestic ethnic groups. Consequently, talk of racial discrimination in the postcolonial period was regarded by those in power as nonsense sowed by provocateurs" (82). By downplaying racial divisions, the Jamaican government apparently hoped to convince the poor and oppressed themselves that it was in their best interests to ignore Rastafarian complaints about injustice and inequality in Jamaica. At the same time, of course, the government hoped to persuade foreign investors that Jamaica was "safe."

Jamaica's print media, especially the national newspaper, the *Daily Gleaner*, led the effort to promote the myth of "Jamaican Exceptionalism." In 1960, the *Gleaner* featured an article by JLP party leader Alexander Bustamante celebrating Jamaica as a country "where races work and live in harmony with ever-increasing respect for each other" (10). In 1963, *Daily Gleaner* columnist William Strong likewise declared that Jamaica was a country where its citizens lived in unity. Asserting that Jamaica's national motto, "Out of Many, One People," reflected this racial harmony, Strong portrayed Jamaica as "neither a black nor a white nor a pink country" but a country where "men may dwell together in unity and good fellowship" (8). As Jamaican writer W. Adolphe Roberts summarized the government's promotion of the myth of Jamaican Exceptionalism in the magazine Pepperpot in 1965, the government considered it "mischievous to argue that Jamaica is a Negro country" just as it would be "patently silly to say that it is Aryan. *Jamaica is itself*" (53).

A second tactic of counter-persuasion was to discredit the Rastafarian movement itself with ridicule and fear appeals. Since 1834, the *Gleaner* has had complete control over Jamaica's print media. While not owned by the government, the paper traditionally had supported the ruling class. Indeed only the middle and upper classes could afford to buy and read the newspaper (A. Brown, "Mass Communication" 303). According to Aggrey Brown, the *Gleaner* did not have to "consciously discriminate between classes" because "those who could buy and read the newspaper were already . . . class determined" ("Mass Communication" 303).

It comes as no surprise, then, that the *Gleaner* historically supported conservative parties and policies and was critical of many Jamaican "radicals," including black nationalist Marcus Garvey (A. Brown, "Mass Media" 21). As the Rastafarian movement grew and spread in the 1960s, the *Gleaner* naturally condemned the Rastafarian movement, characterizing its followers as "lazy" and unproductive. In a 1960 editorial, "Rascally Rastafarians," for example, columnist Clinton Parchment wrote of the Rastas as "lazy, ganja-smoking good-for-nothings" who have an "aversion to work" (8). In another caustic editorial, "The Rastafarian Psychology," Parchment denounced the movement as a collection of "mental juvenile delinquents with no will" to work (9). The *Gleaner* also printed letters supposedly from ordinary Jamaican citizens to support the newspaper's characterization of the movement. One H. M. Howell, for example, contested the link between Jamaica's national hero Marcus Garvey and the Rastafarian movement. Howell argued that Garvey "would be the most miserable man in the world, had he lived to see a thing like this, which is born out of laziness, as he was a hater of lazy men" (8).

Yet even as the government condemned Rastas for their laziness, the paper also cultivated fears of a Rastafarian conspiracy to violently overthrow the Jamaican government. In a 1959 editorial, for example, Clinton Parchment condemned the Rastafarians for their "violen[ce]" and "villainy" ("Bearding" 8). In his 1963 column, "You Can Quote Me," William Strong warned that "misguided" black nationalism could have disastrous consequences. Strong wrote, "[U]tter rubbish born out of ignorance and being aggressively nurtured to a danger point, . . . this attitude can do untold harm to the spirit of unity" in Jamaica (10). In another editorial, Strong warned Jamaican citizens to protect this "nice little island" from degenerating into "social barbarism" (8). However, Parchment's fear appeals perhaps best summarized the *Gleaner*'s attitude toward the Rastafarians: "[The Rastafarians are] a highly dangerous nucleus, capable of exploding in any crisis. Any natural catastrophe might turn them into murderous looters, any time of tension into sparkers of civil disorder, any period of acute criminality into a reservoir of more criminals" ("Rascally" 8).

The *Gleaner* often attributed the threat posed by the Rastafarians to their use of marijuana. In a 1961 column, "Get It Right," columnist Matthew Strong argued that the "aggressiveness" of the Rastafarians were "intimately wrapped up with ganja smoking." Marijuana, according to Strong, "breeds irritation which flares up all the time in 'incidents'" (12). After the 1963 Rose Hall incident, in which several Rastafarians allegedly burned down a gas station and killed eight people, the *Gleaner* attributed the killings to the fact that a "half dozen persons of Rastafarian persuasion got themselves hopped up on ganja" ("Rose Hall" 10). The editors at the *Gleaner* often featured sensational headlines of Rastafarian murders, defiance of the drug laws, and squatting on government property.

These efforts at counter-persuasion aimed to divide and polarize Jamaica's dominant classes from the Rastafarians. According to the national mythology of the dominant classes, Jamaicans valued work, while Rastafarians lingered on the streets in "limbo." "Respectable" Jamaicans were law-abiding citizens; in contrast, Rastafarians engaged in illegal land seizures and "fanatical" marijuana smoking. While Jamaicans were Christians who believed in the "God above," Rastafarians blasphemously believed the emperor of Ethiopia, Haile Selassie, was the "living" African god. In short, Rastafarians were everything "real" Jamaicans were not, and they threatened the prosperity and peace of all Jamaicans.

Like the government's strategy of evasion, however, the strategy of counter-persuasion ultimately failed to disarm the Rastafarian movement. During the 1960s, the realities of gang warfare and national strikes effectively countered "Jamaican Exceptionalism." Likewise, the *Gleaner's* seemingly exaggerated and contradictory portrayal of the Rastafarians as "lazy revolutionaries" failed to provide a convincing description of the Rastafarians that Jamaicans encountered in their everyday lives. Seemingly unable to stem the Rastafarian's growing political consciousness and widening popularity, the Jamaican government and its surrogates thus sometimes turned to yet another, still more aggressive strategy of social control: the strategy of coercion. Yet, again, the strategy did not work exactly as planned.

THE STRATEGY OF COERCION

When milder strategies prove unsuccessful in counteracting the agitation of a social movement, establishments typically resort to a strategy of "coercion" (Stewart, Smith, and Denton 153). This strategy may remain largely rhetorical—what Herbert W. Simons referred to as "coercive persuasion" ("Persuasion in Social" 232). Simons coined the term "coercive persuasion" because he believed "elements of persuasion and inducement or persuasion and constraint are generally manifested in the same act" (*Persuasion* 253). Or it can escalate to more physical tactics, such as firebombing homes or physically attacking demonstrators (Stewart, Smith, and Denton 153). The tactics of coercion also may include restrictive legislation, imprisonment, or even assassination (Stewart, Smith, and Denton 153–4). According to Stewart, Smith, and Denton, the strategy of coercion aims to isolate "leaders from followers" and to portray social movement leaders as "common criminals and dangerous social deviants" (155). In Jamaica, however, the coercion was often directed against ordinary Rastafarians rather than their leaders, and when the government did try to target the leadership, the diverse and decentralized nature of the movement rendered the strategies ineffective.

While no existing study has examined comprehensively the use of coercion to suppress the Rastafarians, several studies have suggested how Jamaican authorities used physical intimidation against the movement. In the 1960 study, *Report on the Rastafari Movement in Kingston, Jamaica*, the authors reported that police routinely employed physical force and intimidation, including the shaving of dreadlocks, to punish the Rastafarians (36). In another study by religious studies scholar Neville Callam, it was reported that Jamaican security forces had infiltrated Rastafarian meetings, arrested members, and raided and damaged Rastafarian homes (39). In her book on the Rastafarian movement, sociologist Anita M. Waters reported that police harassment had long been a common tactic used to control the movement. In one case, according to Waters, police deliberately set fire to "cave dwellings" near Wareika Hills, killing one Rastafarian (104). In the most comprehensive study of Jamaican political violence, Terry Lacey reported that Jamaica's underpaid and overworked security forces often used excessive force to subdue the Jamaican poor, including the Rastafarians (116–18).

The Rastafarians themselves complained often about police brutality in such forums as the black nationalist newspaper *Abeng*. One Jamaican man, who claimed to have witnessed police harassing Rastafarians for selling brooms, told *Abeng* that police "hit the Bretherens with their batons. One burly member of the pack began tearing the Bretherens' [sic] hair from their faces and head while his cronies all with guardsticks, after [sic] keep on to batter the Bretheren" (Grant 2). In another incident reported by *Abeng*, police allegedly raided and burned down a Rastafarian hut in Morant Bay, the parish capital of St. Thomas. Accused of illegally squatting on government land, Rastafarian fishermen, according to the report, were "left destitute by this vicious attack on their persons and the destruction of their property" ("Police Destroy" 1).

The Jamaican government backed up this intimidation and violence with legislation making it easier to arrest and to imprison Rastafarians. Most notably, according to Nettleford, the government established a convenient rationale for coercion against the movement by declaring ganja a "dangerous drug and all users a danger to the established social order" (*Identity* 79). In 1964, Jamaica's Parliament passed amendments to the 1948 Dangerous Drugs Law, implementing tougher marijuana laws (Fraser 373). Prior to the amendments, a first conviction for selling, cultivating, or possessing ganga resulted in a twelve-month sentence and a monetary fine. Under the new legislation, a first conviction for selling or cultivating was now a minimum sentence of five years; possession of marijuana resulted in an eighteen-month sentence (Fraser 373). In the 1960s, the Jamaican government implemented a wide-ranging program to enforce its tough new attitude toward the marijuana trade. The police used helicopters to locate marijuana fields, and monetary rewards were offered for information leading to the arrest and conviction of persons trafficking the drug (Nettleford, *Identity* 81). The result, as H. Aubrey Fraser has noted, was that the number of cases reported involving drugs skyrocketed from 950 in 1966 to 2,154 in 1971 (376). While the drugs seized during this period included cocaine, the majority of the drug arrests involved marijuana. The high number of marijuana arrests confirmed Horace Campbell's observation that the "war on Rastas and the war on ganja became one" (*Rasta* 107).

Writing in the May 17, 1969, issue of *Abeng*, a Rastafarian, Pops Kassim, suggested how police often used the drug laws as an excuse to harass and intimidate the Rastafarians. According to Kassim, one group of Rastafarians and other ghetto youths, presumably suspected of being "ganja-smokers" were lined up in the street and publicly flogged (3). Since no arrests were made in this particular case, it appears that the goal was simply to intimidate and publicly humiliate the Rastafarians. Their alleged use of drugs served as an excuse for such actions.

Typically, the strategy of coercion is aimed not at the lowly followers of a movement but at its leadership. In Jamaica, however, efforts to target leadership of the movement proved difficult, since the Rastafarians had no single, identifiable leader nor even a single type of leader whose removal might have crippled the movement.

On some occasions, police targeted such political activists as Claudius Henry, the man who was first imprisoned in 1959 for fraud and disturbing the peace as a result of his failed scheme to repatriate his brethren to Africa. Supposedly suspected of plotting to overthrow the government, Henry's headquarters were subsequently raided on at least two separate occasions, in 1960 and 1968, and Henry was imprisoned on numerous occasions. Yet as a political activist, perhaps even a violent "revolutionary," Henry did not speak for most Rastafarians, perhaps not even for a sizable minority. His arrest and imprisonment did little to stem the growth of Rastafari in the 1960s.

A second spokesperson for the Rastafarian movement targeted by the government, UWI professor Walter Rodney, likewise did not really speak for the broad spectrum of Rastafarians in Jamaica. Deported by the government in 1968, his "crime" had been to champion the intellectual doctrines of the Black Power movement on the UWI campus. Some "religious" Rastafarians, however, did not view Rodney as a "leader," since Rodney himself critiqued the movement's idealization of Africa. More important, some "religious" Rastafarians could not identify with Rodney's attempt to affiliate Rastafari with Jamaica's Black Power movement. Still other Rastafarians rejected Rodney's efforts to "intellectualize" the movement. The Rastafarian's newspaper, the *Rasta Voice*, dubbed academics like Rodney "false" revolutionaries (I Ras I 5). For these reasons, Rodney's deportation in 1968 did little to disrupt the movement.

The Jamaican government and its surrogates also targeted some of the more outspoken reggae musicians, apparently convinced that they had become "leaders" of the movement. Bob Marley's biographer, Timothy White, claimed that by the mid-1960s, it was rumored that the police wanted the Wailers "behind bars" (221). In 1967, the Wailers' percussionist Bunny Wailer was arrested for allegedly possessing marijuana. Wailer served a fourteen-month sentence that included hard labor. Peter Tosh, another member of the Wailers, received a brief jail sentence for his participation in the anti-Rhodesian demonstrations in Jamaica in 1968. Reggae artist Fred Hibbert of the reggae group the Maytals composed several "prison" songs while serving a twelve-month sentence for possession of marijuana, including the song entitled "54–46 (That's My Number)" that recalled Hibbert's own mistreatment in jail. These imprisonments did not, however, silence the music. Indeed, they only turned a number of reggae musicians into martyrs for the cause and provided still more evidence of the injustices about which they sang.

Between 1959 and 1971, the Jamaican government's coercive tactics thus did little to disrupt or suppress the Rastafarian movement. Therefore, the Jamaican government turned to one last strategy commonly used to control social movements—the strategy of "adjustment." Yet again, however, the strategy did not seem to be successful.

THE STRATEGY OF ADJUSTMENT

The strategy of "adjustment," according to Stewart, Smith, and Denton, "involves making some concessions to a social movement while not accepting the movement's demands or goals" (155). According to Bowers, Ochs, and Jensen, the tactics of "adjustment" may include such "token" concessions as changing the name of a regulatory agency to project the illusion of a "real adjustment in an establishment's structure, personnel, or ideology" (60). It also might include sacrificing personnel unpopular with the movement or incorporating personnel of the movement itself into the hierarchy of the "establishment." Finally, the established authorities might accept some of the means of agitation, allowing the agitators to protest within certain safe boundaries rather than "openly challenge them" (Bowers, Ochs, and Jensen 62). In many respects, the strategy of adjustment only addresses "superficial elements of conflict and seldom results in permanent solutions to social unrest and movement demands" (Stewart, Smith, and Denton 155). Nevertheless, it often proves effective because agitators can "see some visible effect of their efforts" (Bowers, Ochs, and Jensen 63).

The Jamaican government's adjustment to the demands of the Rastafari was evident in two major ways. First, the government allowed—even welcomed—a visit to Jamaica by Rastafarian godhead, Haile Selassie, in 1966. Second, the Jamaican ruling class accepted certain means of protest, most notably by allowing supposed Rastafarians to editorialize in the national newspaper, the *Daily Gleaner*. Both of these "adjustments" were aimed at appeasing and pacifying the Rastafarians, but again they were less than entirely successful. Instead of pacifying the Rastafarians, Selassie's visit only turned more of them toward political activism, while editorials by supposed Rastafarian spokespersons did not represent the views of most Rastafarians.

In April 1966, Ethiopian emperor Haile Selassie made his first official visit to Jamaica. Since the Mission to Africa committee visited the African continent in 1961, the Jamaican government has routinely invited African dignitaries to Jamaica (Nettleford, *Identity* 61–2). The Jamaican government invited Selassie to Jamaica when they realized that the emperor had plans to visit Trinidad and Tobago. During the visit, Selassie met with government officials, addressed both houses of the Jamaican Parliament, and was awarded an honorary Doctor of Laws by the University of the West Indies (T. White 212). Selassie also allegedly met with Rastafarian "leaders."

Rather than simply appeasing the Rastafarians, however, Selassie's visit empowered them by highlighting the strength and popularity of Rastafari as a grassroots social movement. Selassie's visit drew the largest Rastafarian contingent assembled in Jamaica's history, and for the first time, the Jamaican government and the public realized that the Rastafarians were more than just a tiny cult of drug addicts and religious fanatics. During a 1994 interview, Jamaican anthropologist Barry Chevannes recalled the impact of Selassie's visit on the Rastafarian movement: "What we had was a movement which had spread among the masses, and so the rest of the [Jamaican] population was not aware of this, and they were totally taken by surprise." Leonard Barrett, a noted scholar of the Rastafarian movement, called Selassie's visit one of the major turning points in the Rastafarian's "rountinization" or "legitimization" as a social movement in Jamaica (161).

More important, Selassie ignited the already growing political consciousness of the Rastafarian movement with his decree that the Rastafarians ought to seek "liberation" in Jamaica before "repatriation" to Africa. In the aftermath of Selassie's pronouncement, the Rastafarian movement formed a tenuous alliance with Jamaica's Black Power movement, published its first newspaper, the *Rasta Voice,* and became more identified with the increasingly politicized lyrics of Jamaica's popular music. In effect, the government's attempt to "adjust" to Rastafarian concerns by inviting Selassie to visit did not merely fail to appease the movement; the whole strategy backfired. Instead of mollifying the dissidents, the visit became the single most important event in the politicization of Rastafari.

In a second adjustment tactic, the *Daily Gleaner* published letters from Rastafarian "leaders." Samuel Brown, identified by the *Gleaner* as a spokesperson for the "Rastafarian Movement in Jamaica," was one of the more "political" and outspoken of these Rastafarian "leaders" to publish in the *Gleaner*. During the 1960s, Brown wrote several letters to the paper, defending the Rastafarians from detractors and clarifying the movement's goals. In 1960, Brown responded to criticism that the Rastafarians were "fanatics" by accusing the dominant classes of "immoralit[ies]" and complaining that the dominant classes' "deeds of shame lie covered" (8). In 1966, Brown also responded to charges that Rastafarians were an "undisciplined crowd" during Selassie's 1966 visit to Jamaica. Brown wrote instead of the "exemplary conduct of the representatives of the much maligned Rastafarians" (10). Brown was one of the movement's most prolific letter writers, and the *Gleaner*'s decision to publish his letters made it appear that Brown's "political" views represented the views of most Rastafarians. Of course, Brown did not, in fact, speak for all Rastafarians. In fact, most "religious" Rastafarians rejected Brown's aspirations to involve the movement in Jamaica's political institutions. For example, when Brown ran as an independent candidate (under the Black Man's Party) in the 1961 elections, he could not gain "substantial support" even from "the majority of the Rastafarian brethren" (Nagashima 26). Apparently, Brown was especially unpopular among politically passive, religiously oriented Rastafarians. After the election, some even denounced him as too "radical" to lead the movement (Barrett 152).

The strategy of adjustment, like all of the strategies of control employed by the Jamaican government in the 1960s, thus proved basically unsuccessful. It did little to stem the increased political activism and growing popularity of the Rastafarian movement. Perhaps, these strategies failed because the Jamaican government never developed a clear, unified strategy but rather responded to particular events with a variety of different tactics.

Beyond the Jamaican government's sometimes clumsy implementation of the various strategies of social control, there may be additional reasons for their failures—reasons rooted in the unique characteristics of the

Rastafarian movement. First, the ideological and organizational nature of the Rastafarian movement rendered many control strategies ineffective. Focusing upon individual, spiritual concerns, and lacking clearly identifiable leadership and an organizational hierarchy, Rastafari could not be controlled as easily as the typical social movement. More important, Rastafari was unique in its growing association with the popular music of Jamaica. To effectively counter the Rastafarian movement, the Jamaican government had to become, in effect, critic and censor of Jamaica's most popular forms of entertainment and culture. By 1971, the government still had yet to devise an effective strategy for dealing with the increasingly anti-government messages of Jamaica's most popular musical forms.

The development of "international reggae" after 1971 made the government's task even more difficult. As the movement gained credibility not only in Jamaica but around the world, it became increasingly difficult to ignore or suppress the movement. With the release of the reggae soundtrack *The Harder They Come* and the Wailers' *Catch a Fire*, reggae attracted international attention, especially on U.S. college campuses. At the same time, the PNP candidate for prime minister, Michael Manley, began expressing publicly his sympathy for the movement and hiring reggae musicians to play at political rallies. As we will see, these events created new possibilities and problems for the Rastafarian movement.

Part Two

(1972–1980)

Chapter Five

INTERNATIONAL REGGAE

Popularization and Polarization of Rastafari

> Not everybody who dreads their hair is a true Rasta. Some of these guys
> talk about how they are a dread and a Rastaman, but they are using it as a
> disguise. Rastafari business isn't what you have on your head; it's what you
> have in your heart.
>
> —dance hall artist Cutty Ranks

After a decade of struggle against an increasingly repressive Jamaica
Labour Party (JLP), Jamaica's poor and dissident groups embraced the can-
didacy of People's National Party (PNP) leader Michael Manley, the son of
former Prime Minister Norman Manley, for prime minister in 1972. During the national election campaign, Manley attempted to appeal to the
Rastafarians and Jamaica's Black Power movement. Manley even adopted
the biblical name "Joshua" and promised the Jamaican people deliverance
from oppression. Two years after winning the election, Manley formally
declared Jamaica a "democratic socialist" country. Democratic socialism

promised a redistribution of wealth in Jamaica and independence from foreign control (Panton 41).

Instead of prosperity, however, the Manley reforms created the worst economic conditions in Jamaica in more than thirty years. An international oil crisis, continuing high unemployment, and inflation eroded Manley's "politics of equality." Manley's last ditch efforts to revive Jamaica's deteriorating economy during his second term failed, and the Jamaican voters elected JLP leader Edward Seaga as the country's new prime minister in 1980.

Meanwhile, reggae music became more popular than ever. Promoted by Island Records President Chris Blackwell and popularized by reggae star Bob Marley, reggae attracted international attention from American and European musicians, rock critics, and fans around the world. This new international reggae actually continued to sound many of the same radical themes as early reggae. As Manley's reforms failed to bring prosperity and peace to Jamaica's underclass, reggae remained a voice of protest. Historically, political—and especially radically political—music was considered less commercially viable. In the case of international reggae, however, U.S. record companies successfully marketed reggae as a new "rebel music" in hopes that it would appeal to white American college students and European youths.

All of these developments created new and intriguing dilemmas for the Rastafarian movement. On one hand, reggae's international popularity increased the visibility and popularity of the Rastafarian movement around the world. As the most visible and prominent advertiser for the movement, reggae spread the Rastafarian gospel to the four corners of the globe. As rock critics Stephen Davis and Peter Simon have observed, reggae propelled "the Rasta cosmology into the middle of the planet's cultural arenas, and suddenly people want to know what all the chanting and praying and obsessive smoking of herb [marijuana] are all about" (*Reggae Bloodlines* 63).

On the other hand, international reggae also exacerbated the split between "religious" and "political" Rastafarians. While more traditional, religious Rastafarians seemed appalled by what they considered the commercialization and secularization of the movement, more politically oriented Rastafarians hoped to exploit reggae's new popularity to further the cause. In addition, the popularity of reggae spawned a number of pseudo-Rastafarian groups, who imitated the cultural trappings of Rastafari—the dreadlocks, the ganja smoking, and the lingo—without embracing its larger religious and ideological tenets. In effect, the commercialization of reggae music, in the view of more traditional Rastafarians at least, trivialized and degraded the movement. Because the popularity of the music was associated with the movement, the movement itself seemed to some to become more of a "cultural fad" than a serious religious and/or political movement.

Reggae reflected this continued political turmoil in Jamaica, even as it was transformed from an obscure "third-world" music to an international musical phenomenon. Lyrically, reggae songs continued to critique Jamaica's social and economic conditions, including unemployment, inadequate housing, and political violence. Yet, unlike early reggae, international reggae reflected more awareness of international issues, especially political turmoil in Zimbabwe and South Africa. In addition, some U.S. record companies modified reggae's sound to appeal more to white audiences. The result was a new international reggae that remained a voice of protest but which broadened its concerns to more universal and international issues and which had a more polished, more commercial sound. While spreading the Rastafarian message to the international community, this "new" reggae exacerbated the rift between political and religious Rastafarians in Jamaica. Inspiring a new wave of secular Rastafarian groups, as well as the rise of a middle-class Rastafarian intelligentsia and pseudo-Rastafarian groups, international reggae brought many new "supporters" into the movement. Yet those supporters had very little in common with traditional Rastafarians. The results were new tensions and divisions within the Rastafarian movement.

JAMAICA: MICHAEL MANLEY, DEMOCRATIC SOCIALISM, AND THE POLITICS OF IDEALISM

During the 1972 national election campaign, PNP candidate Michael Manley pulled out all the political stops. Appealing directly to Jamaica's Rastafarian community, Manley adopted the biblical name "Joshua" and displayed a "magical" walking stick (dubbed the "Rod of Correction") allegedly given to him by Haile Selassie during Manley's 1969 visit to Ethiopia. Tapping into the island's burgeoning popular culture, Manley hired reggae musicians to play at political rallies. In *Jamaica's Michael Manley: The Great Transformation* (1972–92), public policy expert David Panton credited Manley's victory to his oratorical skills, personal charisma, and ability to bring the poor into the political process (33). After winning a landslide victory, Manley told the *Daily Gleaner*, "I hope that I will be in a position to heal some of the bitter divisions that have entered into our Jamaican life, because I feel that the one thing that a country like Jamaica needs is tremendous goodwill and love" (qtd. in "Manley Leads" 1).

For the next two years, Manley enacted legislation consistent with his campaign pledges. Manley lowered the voting age to eighteen, established sugar cooperatives, and supported a bauxite levy in 1974 that helped Jamaica offset higher energy costs due to the international oil crisis of the early 1970s (Manley, *Jamaica* 39–57). Manley also established a land-lease program that made government lands available to farmers, created crash programs to boost employment, offered free secondary education to all Jamaican citizens, and nationalized all foreign-owned electric and telephone services (Payne 67–8). Manley's policies, in his own words, were designed to shift the "power away from the wealthy apex towards the democratic base" (*Jamaica* 87).

Manley avoided specific proposals during the 1972 campaign, but in 1974 he unveiled his vision of democratic socialism to the Jamaican public. Democratic socialism would, according to Manley, provide an alternative to Puerto Rico's capitalist model and Cuba's Communist philosophy (Panton 39). Democratic socialism promised independence from foreign control, greater access to social programs, new allegiances with other "third-world" nations, and a variety of economic reforms (Panton 41). Depicting democratic socialism as both an economic and a "moral" policy, Manley believed the "world must be consciously organized to provide equality of opportunity and social justice for all people" (qtd. in "PM Lists" 1).

Two dramatic economic developments, however, destroyed Manley's socialist dream. The international oil crisis of 1973–1974 virtually crippled Jamaica's economy. Jamaica's costs for imported oil climbed from J$65 million in 1973 to J$177 million in 1974 (Panton 37). While oil prices soared, Jamaica's traditional foreign-exchange earner, bauxite, declined in both production and exportation. According to the *Economic and Social Survey Jamaica, 1975*, Jamaica's bauxite production fell by 25 percent, and exports of bauxite declined by 31 percent (i).

Reeling from the economic slump, Manley found a scapegoat in the United States government, which opposed his new socialist experiment. As Manley geared up for his reelection campaign in 1976, he blamed the Central Intelligence Agency (CIA) for his nation's troubles, suggesting that a CIA conspiracy was at work against his reelection.[1] Manley would later write in his memoirs, *Jamaica: Struggle in the Periphery:* "I have no doubt that the CIA was active in Jamaica that year and was working through its own agents to destablise us" (140).

Nevertheless, Manley was reelected in 1976 in one of Jamaica's bloodiest political elections. From January to May, an estimated one hundred people died in politically motivated violence (Waters 144). The Orange Street Massacre of May 1976 was among the worst incidents. In retaliation for a gang murder, a rival gang set fire to a tenement building, killing eleven and leaving five hundred homeless (Waters 145). In an even more bizarre event, six suspected JLP hitmen stormed into musician Bob Marley's house in early December and wounded several people, including Marley, his wife, Rita Marley, and Don Taylor, the band's manager. In response to this surge of violence, Manley exploded: "[V]iolence in our society is the nation's greatest problem. It must be stamped out" ("Curfews" 19).

Manley devised various measures to curb Kingston's escalating urban violence. In January 1976, Manley created community defense groups called "Home Guard[s]" (Waters 145). The Home Guard task force trained citizens to protect their own communities (Manley, *Jamaica* 85). In June of 1976, Manley declared a national state of emergency in Jamaica which lasted for one year (Manley, *Jamaica* 141–2). While Jamaica was under a state of emergency, Manley instructed his security forces to detain political thugs and JLP leaders suspected of treason. One JLP member, Pearnel Charles, was detained for ten months and wrote about his prison experience in *Detained*.

By April 1977, Jamaica's economy was in shambles. Unemployment had skyrocketed to 24.6 percent (*Economic and Social Survey Jamaica, 1977* 466). International banks stopped extending new loans to the country (Panton 63). Jamaica's civil unrest persuaded potential tourists to seek alternative vacation spots (Panton 60). Jamaica also suffered from a "flight of capital" as an estimated 300 million (U.S.) dollars left the island illegally (Manley, *Jamaica* 151). Political scientist Anthony Payne assessed Jamaica's growing economic crisis: "For ordinary Jamaicans, the reforms of the Manley government had produced a severe decline in living standards, worse unemployment, acute shortages of basic goods in the shops, and a mood of depression that pervaded the whole economy and society" (79–80).

From 1977 to 1980, Manley reluctantly accepted loan agreements from the International Monetary Fund (IMF) to reverse Jamaica's economic slide. In retrospect, Manley claimed the agreements were "one of the most savage packages ever imposed on any client government by the IMF" (*Jamaica* 160). The economic packages forced Jamaica to devalue its dollar and agree to budget cuts and a mandatory cap on wage settlements (Manley, *Jamaica* 160).[2] Manley admitted that the IMF agreements were "one of the most bitter, traumatic experiences of my public life" (*Life and Debt*). By 1979, Manley was so distressed over Jamaica's economic decline, according to his own memoirs, that he contemplated "resigning either on behalf of the government or personally" (166).

During Manley's last years in office, the *Daily Gleaner*, according to Manley, turned against him (*Jamaica* 134). Denouncing Manley's political leadership, several *Gleaner* editorials portrayed him as an incompetent idealist who had defaulted on his political promises. Writing in the January 11, 1980 edition, Thomas Trumann editorialized that Manley had caused "destruction and devastation on the country" (6). *Gleaner* political columnist Colin Gregory called for Manley's resignation:

> Mr. Manley keeps hoping to lead us to the promised land but continues walking up and down the shore of the Red Sea hoping that, like Moses, he can persuade the waters to roll back and provide passage for Jamaicans. Maybe he once thought that some great socialist country would perform that miracle for us but even he must know by now that none is coming forward to do that. And don't ask me to explain to you why Moses could perform that miracle and "Joshua" Manley can't do it. (6)

By the spring of 1980, Manley's political career was virtually over. From February to October 1980, 750 Jamaicans died in political violence (Waters 199). In June 1980, there was a failed coup attempt by supporters of the JLP ("JDF" 1). Bringing about his own political demise, Manley called for early elections in October 1980. Manley himself looked for a vote of confidence, but instead the Jamaican people elected JLP member Edward Seaga as the new prime minister.

REGGAE MUSIC IN THE 1970S: "BUBBLING ON THE TOP 100"

Since the inception of ska in the late 1950s, U.S. and British record companies had been attempting to market Jamaican music to international audiences. While most of these early attempts failed, a few reggae musicians managed to achieve some international success. For example, in 1964, Millie Small's song "My Boy Lollipop" sold over six million copies and became an international hit (Jones 58). In 1967, Desmond Dekker's song "007" made the top twenty in England (Jones 58). By the late 1960s, however, most rock fans continued to ignore reggae, presumably because of the music's seemingly "'repetitive'" and "'boring'" rhythms (Jones 61). As sociologist Simon Jones has observed, the "widespread hostility towards reggae within the rock market constituted a major marketing problem for those recording companies seeking to 'break' Jamaican music to a wider audience" (61).

In 1972, however, Chris Blackwell, president of Island Records, came up with a scheme to market a "new" and "improved" reggae to American college students and European youths. Casting Jamaica's leading reggae group, the Wailers, as "rock stars," Blackwell launched a massive campaign to promote the Wailers' new album, *Catch a Fire* (Jones 62). Blackwell's marketing genius created "a new and larger audience for reggae," eventually opening "the possibilities of mass white consumption" of reggae (Jones 61–2). Many other reggae artists followed in the Wailers' footsteps, and, by the mid-1970s, there was a sudden explosion in reggae's international popularity.

Defying conventional wisdom in the music industry, Blackwell and his imitators successfully marketed this "radical" political music, not by toning down its politics, but by actually celebrating the ganja-smoking Rastafarian as a universal symbol of rebellion and protest. Blackwell, in particular, was determined to underscore "the social and political content" of reggae music (Hebdige, *Cut* 79).

Protest Lyrics

International reggae remained a radical political music. Lyrically, international reggae exposed and critiqued the deplorable living conditions in Jamaica's slums (e.g., Toots and the Maytals' "Time Tough"). In addition, reggae songs such as "Catch a Fire" (*Catch a Fire*) and "Slavery Days" (*100th Anniversary*) continued to ground such critiques in historical memories of slavery, conjuring up images of slave ships, plantations, manacles, and whips. Reggae songs also continued to denounce "Babylon" (i.e., police, CIA, Jamaican government), praise Jah, the vengeful God, and encourage belief in the dream of repatriation (e.g., Bunny Wailer's "Dream Land" [*Blackheart Man*]). However, there were at least three changes in international reggae that universalized its themes of protest and repositioned the Rastafarians as part of a larger, more "universal," pan-African movement.

First, Marcus Garvey, who represented a defiant symbol of black nationalism for blacks throughout the world, became a more prominent figure in international reggae. Burning Spear's first two international releases, *Marcus Garvey* and *Garvey's Ghost*, celebrated the life of Garvey, while "Black Starliner Must Come," by a reggae group called Culture, lamented that Garvey's ships still had not arrived: "We're waiting on an opportunity / We're waiting on the black starliner / For the black starliner shall come" (*Two Sevens Clash*).

Second, international reggae cast Rastafarians, not "Jamaicans," as Africans who happened to live in Jamaica. In a blunt statement of African nationality, for example, Peter Tosh sang: "Don't care where you come from / So long as you are a black man / You're an African" (*Equal Rights*). In "War," an adaptation of a 1968 speech by Haile Selassie, Bob Marley like-wise depicted Rastafarians as "Africans" fighting for "the victory of good over evil" (*Rastaman Vibration*). Finally, Marley's "Africa Unite" urged all blacks to unite with "Africans abroad" (*Survival*).

Finally, there was a greater interest among reggae artists in the social and political issues on the African continent. Black Uhuru's song, "World Is Africa," (*Sinsemilla*) typified this new international focus, as did Peter Tosh's second solo album, *Equal Rights*, which included a song entitled "Apartheid." Tosh would even title one of his later albums *Mama Africa*, while Bob Marley dedicated one of his albums, *Survival*, to black freedom fighters in Zimbabwe. The album's most arresting songs, "Zimbabwe," "Ambush in the Night," "Africa Unite," and "So Much Trouble in the World" all discussed African tribal warfare and apartheid. In "Zimbabwe," Marley celebrated the "Natty Dread in Zimbabwe," ready to "mash it up." In "Africa Unite," Marley claimed that Jamaicans and Africans were unit-ed as "children of the Higher Man." The songs urged African nations to unite for the "benefit of your people" (*Survival*).

According to speech communication scholar Ralph E. Knupp, protest songs are particularly effective if the songs contain a high degree of ambiguity and appeal to a listener's experience and social setting (386). While many of reggae's themes grew out of poverty and oppression in Jamaica, they also spoke to the experiences of people around the world. Themes such as "poverty," "oppres-sion," "resistance," and "redemption" are universal themes of protest. Kenneth M. Bilby, noted scholar on Caribbean music, observed that reggae's lyrics had a "general ideological appeal" based on the Rastafarian movement's "rebellious, anti-authority" stance and "'utopian' thrust" ("Black Thoughts" 203).

97

Musical Instrumentation and Image Creation

Ultimately, however, international reggae's appeal to international audiences may have had more to do with changes in the images of reggae artists, the packaging of the albums, and the sound of the music itself. In his efforts to market the Wailers, for example, Blackwell first molded the Wailers' image into that of a rock-and-roll group. While reggae "groups" typically had consisted of a loose collection of singers and hired studio musicians, Blackwell promoted the Wailers as a stable, self-contained "band"—much like the Rolling Stones or Led Zeppelin.

Second, Blackwell led a new trend among Jamaica's record producers toward original, thematic, and full-length LP (long-play) albums, again following the lead of rock-and-roll groups. Previously, Jamaica's record producers had distributed mostly singles or cheaply produced compilations of "'greatest hits'" (Jones 62–3).

Finally, those albums came packaged in glossy, well-produced jackets promoting the image of the rebellious, ganja-smoking Rastafarian. On the back cover of the Wailers' 1973 album *Burnin'*, for example, Marley was pictured smoking a twelve-inch spliff, or marijuana cigarette. On Peter Tosh's 1976 album, *Legalize It*, the singer was photographed crouched down in a ganja field. Reggae album covers also emphasized the Rastafarian's symbols of black defiance: the dreadlocks and the display of the Ethiopian colors of red, green, and gold. The cover of the Wailers' 1980 album *Uprising*, featured a drawing of Bob Marley, along with the album's title in red, and a background of green mountains and a gold sun.

While most of the major instrumental innovations of international reggae were established during the early reggae period (Grass 47), international reggae was marked by a more sophisticated and polished studio sound. Most early reggae songs were recorded in "primitive" studios in Jamaica. International reggae, however, generally was recorded in state-of-the-art studios in the United States or Great Britain. According to sociologist Simon Jones, this helped to undermine "the common accusation made by rock fans that reggae was a music of 'inferior' quality" (64). In the first attempt to reverse this trend, Chris Blackwell took the Wailers' instrumental tracks for *Catch a Fire*, previously recorded in Jamaica, and remixed, edited, and mastered the tracks in a London studio (Jones 64). Rock critics Ed Ward, Geoffrey Stokes, and Ken Tucker highlighted the dramatic change in reggae's new sound: *Catch a Fire* was "revolutionary, . . . far superior in its *technology* than most other reggae records" (emphasis mine) (541).

U.S. record producers also manipulated the instrumentation in reggae arrangements to create a lighter, "softer" reggae. Some U.S. record producers would de-emphasize reggae's dominant instruments, the electric bass guitar and drums, and push the keyboard and electric guitar to the front of the mix. In 1980, Jamaican dub poet and musician Linton Kwesi Johnson provided a clear rationale for the systematic manipulation of the reggae sound: "[There was] the belief that the hard Jamaican sound, with the emphasis on the drum and the bass, would not be as accessible to the non-Jamaican listener as a lighter sounding production would be" ("Some Thoughts" 58).

To appeal to international audiences, reggae musicians also incorporated familiar genres of American music into the reggae arrangement. During the remixing of the Wailers' *Catch a Fire*, for example, Blackwell overdubbed traditional rock-and-roll instruments, including lead guitar, keyboard, and synthesizer, using British and American musicians (Jones 64). During the recording of the same album, a session guitarist, Wayne Perkins, also added guitar solos. Throughout their career, the Wailers dabbled in blues ("Talkin' Blues" [*Natty Dread*]), funk ("Could You Be Loved" [*Uprising*]), disco ("Exodus" [*Exodus*]), and folk music ("Redemption Song" [*Uprising*]). Similarly, Toots and the Maytals, in their 1973 *Funky Kingston*, fused R&B and reggae in the album's title song, and even recorded a country song (John Denver's "Country Road") and a rock-and-roll standard (The Kingsmen's "Louie Louie"). In yet another example, Peter Tosh brought a reggae beat to a classic fifties rock-and-roll song, Chuck Berry's "Johnny B. Goode" (*The Toughest*).

In sum, the new international success of reggae music in the 1970s may have been more the result of marketing and changes in its sound than changes in its "message." Reggae's sudden status as an international musical sensation focused unprecedented attention on the Rastafarian movement and exacerbated tensions between more traditional, religious Rastafarians and those with political ambitions. Indeed, the music created whole new groups of supposed Rastafarians apparently attracted to the movement by little more than the image of the "Rastaman" and the music itself.

THE RASTAFARIAN MOVEMENT: "COMING IN FROM THE COLD"

By the mid-1970s, reggae music was widely perceived as "the music of the oppressed in almost every major Black Community not only in the West but [in] Africa also" (Ahkell 15). The fusion of reggae and Rastafari popularized the movement throughout the world. This marriage of "movement" and "music," however, also created a wider division between political and religious Rastafarians, and the emergence of new "secular" Rastafarian groups threatened to turn Rastafari into something of a cultural fad rather than a serious religious movement. Increasingly divorced from the poor Rastafarians in the Jamaican ghettos, the movement became more "secular" and, critics would argue, more preoccupied with superficial symbols rather than genuine religious practices. Attracting middle-class intellectuals, and spawning pseudo-Rastafarian groups, reggae's international popularity was both a blessing and a curse for the Rastafarian movement.

Throughout the world in the 1970s, reggae's new international sound was praised by critics and imitated by other musicians. In 1973, *Time* correspondent Joan Downs described reggae as "lilting pop rock" and called it the "most captivating musical export since steel bands" (79). Writing in a 1974 issue of the entertainment magazine *Sepia*, journalists Barbara and Patrick Salvo similarly praised reggae, claiming that it had "the energy and momentum to get the fans up out of their concert hall seats and dancing in the aisles once again" (37).

American rock stars acknowledged the influence of reggae in their own musical compositions. Blues artist Taj Mahal recorded the Wailers' "Slave Driver," while Barbra Streisand recorded another Wailers' song, "Guava Jelly," for her 1973 *ButterFly* album. Paul Simon, the first white American musician to record a reggae-influenced song—"Mother and Child Reunion"—told *Time* magazine in 1973 that although reggae music is "hard to explain . . . I love it" (qtd. in Downs 79). Of all the American and European musicians influenced by reggae music, rock guitarist Eric Clapton played the foremost role in popularizing reggae in the United States. Clapton's 1974 cover of the Wailers' "I Shot the Sheriff" outsold the original version and became an international hit.

In the United States and Britain, the punk "movement" also had embraced reggae themes by the mid- to late 1970s. The punks, a new generation of disenfranchised working-class whites, identified with reggae's themes of rebellion and alienation. Some punks wore Ethiopian colors and began to use the language of Rastafari (i.e., "Babylon"). Punk groups like the Clash weaved reggae themes into their songs and introduced reggae numbers into their sets. At the same time, Marley recorded a song, "Punky Reggae Party," to acknowledge this meeting of cultures.

In the late 1970s, several reggae artists, including Bob Marley and the Wailers and Jimmy Cliff, toured Africa. In 1979, the Wailers released *Survival*, an album that addressed the political turmoil in Africa. African militants chanted the album's hit song "Zimbabwe" during the civil war in Rhodesia. Writing for the *New Society*, Roy Kerridge claimed "reggae and Marley have made an enormous impression on Africa." The popularity of both reggae and Rastafari in Africa influenced some Africans to "wear dreadlocks, smoke ganja and do their best to imagine that they are Jamaicans" (343).

Although Rastafarian camps had been spotted in Great Britain since the 1950s, by the late 1970s the movement had, in the words of one sympathetic study, "flowered and the wind . . . dispersed the seeds far and wide" (Semaj, "Rastafari" 22). In Japan, a self-proclaimed Rastafarian named Jah Hiro promoted the movement as a spiritual alternative to the "dead" culture of Europe (Eastham 2). The African countries of Zimbabwe and Nigeria sprouted several Rastafarian collectivities, and closer to Jamaica, the Rastafarian presence was strongly felt in the eastern Caribbean countries of Antigua, Barbados, and Trinidad. So common did Rastafarian groups become around the world that Rastafarian scholar Horace Campbell dreamed that the Rastafarian movement eventually could form the basis of a "universal culture" (*Rasta* 234).

While one might think all this attention would be welcomed by Rastafarians, it in fact served to widen the traditional conflict between "religious" and "political" elements of the movement. Over the years, as we have seen, religious and more politically oriented Rastafarians had been split on such issues as repatriation to Africa. Religious Rastafarians now complained that the use of reggae as campaign songs and a source of campaign slogans during the 1972, 1976, and 1980 national elections demeaned the movement. Some traditionalists even believed the movement's involvement in politics was "'satanic' because it has caused divisions and stamped a mark of disgrace on the Rastafarian movement" (Nagashima 26).

Many Rastafarian traditionalists also criticized reggae for commercializing the movement. According to Barbara Lee, a member of the Rastafarian movement, critics were alarmed that reggae musicians were "more concerned with profits, than converts to the cause of Black liberation" (40). Traditionalists ridiculed reggae musicians as international stars who deliberately diluted the Rastafarian message in order to appeal to large, often white audiences. According to sociologist Yoshiko S. Nagashima, some Rastafarians found it "intolerable" that the "distorted artificiality" of international reggae was "accepted as genuine" by so many listeners (181).

Not only did the popularity of reggae contribute to this wider schism, the music also played a significant role in the development of "pseudo-Rastafarian" groups—groups drawn to the movement primarily by its fashions and association with reggae music. In 1977, Cedric Brooks, a noted Jamaican musician, expressed the concern of many more traditional Rastafarians that the movement had become more of a cultural fad than a religion: "People coming into the faith are not really grounded in the hard-core religious philosophy, and some tend to go only by the paraphernalia and outward appearances of the culture" (Brooks 15). According to Bob Marley's biographer Timothy White, by the mid-1970s some middle to upper-class Jamaicans began to embrace Rastafarian fashions while disregarding the movement's "strict dietary rules, the religious beliefs and the humility of the authentic" Rastafarian (259–60). According to cultural critic Dick Hebdige, one Rastafarian raged against these "pseudo-Rastafarians" for "smashing the Father [Haile Selassie] around. . . . They think it's a fashion, you see, but Rasta is not fashion. . . . Rasta is pureness" (qtd. in *Cut* 53). Carolyn Cooper, one of Jamaica's leading experts on Jamaican dancehall music, agreed in a 1994 interview that by the 1990s more and more mainstream Jamaicans had adopted the movement's symbols—Ethiopian colors, dreadlocks—without "necessarily seeing themselves as Rastas."

Even some middle-class intellectuals in Jamaica "converted" to the Rastafarian faith.[3] This too pushed the movement further away from its religious heritage and more into the secular, political realm. Rastafarian Leahcim Semaj was the leading voice for a new wave of Rastafarian intellectuals. Semaj intimated on more than one occasion that traditional non-political Rastafarians would have to "'put-up'" with Rastafarian intellectuals or "cease to visibly identify themselves with Rastafari." They would have to learn to transcend their religious beliefs and embrace "social theory." According to Semaj, Rastafarians needed to become "activists" engaged in creating social theory as a "tool for liberation." The development of a Rastafarian social theory would allow the Rastafarians to share in the "state power" and act as a "vehicle through which the feelings and reality of significant sections from the labor class . . . the ghetto culture . . . can be articulated." Ultimately, a Rastafarian social theory would increase the opportunity for a "revolutionary conflict" in Jamaica ("Inside" 38).

Still other "pseudo-Rastafarian" groups rejected the movement's traditional views altogether. Founded by Jamaican Keith Gordon in the late 1960s, the Ethiopian Zion Coptic Church, for example, was started in Jamaica but relocated to Miami, Florida, in the early 1970s. From the start, the Coptics encouraged American and European whites to join the group. More important, the Coptics denounced their Rastafarian brethren in Jamaica as "ropeheads," repudiated Haile Selassie's divinity, and criticized reggae for promoting lust and violence. Brother Louv, the Coptic's leader, criticized even reggae's most influential star, Bob Marley, for what he considered to be a disservice to the movement:

> Is it Bob Marley who has the song, "I Shot the Sheriff"? To me, that's not a contribution; to me, that's a great damage that can do nothing except inspire violence. Are the followers who follow after him doing anything conscious? I've yet to hear of it. Reggae music is doing a lot of damage to the ganja argument. For when you try to show the non-smoker what ganja is about, they look to the Rasta. (qtd. in Blake 1)

Back in Jamaica, even the *Gleaner* denounced the Coptics as "Star Island hippies" and insisted that neither the "'white rastas' from Miami nor their paid black minions have any authority to speak about Africa where, they say, Rasta originated" (Kitchin, "A People's" 8, 13). Critical of the Coptic's materialism, the *Gleaner* observed "crisp expensive European cars" parked at the Coptic settlement (Ritch, "Middle-Class" 6) and accused the group of acquiring their wealth through shady land deals and drug trafficking (Campbell, *Rasta* 115–16).

Nevertheless, the Coptics provided the most extreme example of what had become a real problem for the Rastafarian movement—the proliferation of "pseudo-Rastafarian" groups claiming to speak for the movement. Typically embracing only the external trappings of Rastafari—the ganja smoking, the dreadlocks, or reggae music itself—these groups threatened to reduce Rastafari to little more than a cultural fad. While never a highly organized movement with strong central leadership, Rastafari became, in the 1970s, even more fragmented, more diverse, and less unified by common religious or political tenets.

While this might have made the movement harder to suppress, it also made it more vulnerable to co-optation and domestication by the new PNP government. In the 1970s, the PNP government no longer even tried to "control" the movement by evading its demands, refuting its claims, or coercing Rastafarians into compliance. Faced with the growing popularity of international reggae, Manley thus turned to a new approach to deal with the movement: co-optation—embracing the movement not only politically, but as Jamaica's new cultural treasure.

Chapter Six

MICHAEL MANLEY AND THE PEOPLE'S NATIONAL PARTY'S CO-OPTATION OF THE RASTAFARI AND REGGAE

[R]eggae artists such as Bob Marley . . . [were] bringing about a
Rastafari Revolution in Jamaica.

—**Barbara Makeda Lee**

During the 1960s, the Jamaican establishment denounced the Rastafarian movement as a scourge of frenzied drug abusers. A decade later,
Jamaica's new prime minister, Michael Manley, expressed sympathy for
the Rastafarian movement, while Jamaica's dominant classes increasingly
embraced the movement as a cultural asset. A curious, often perplexed
international media spotlighted this "new" religious "cult," while a new
generation of academic scholars approached the Rastafarians more sym-
pathetically.[1] Observing these changes, religious studies scholar Neville
Callam concluded in 1980 that for the first time in Jamaica's history,

Rastafari had become "part of the taken-for-granted landscape" (43). Sociologist Klaus de Albuquerque believed that the Rastafarians were as Jamaican as "ackee and salt fish, the national dish of Jamaica" (22). Political scientist Len Garrison's claim that the movement had become accepted in "all corners of the society," while perhaps a bit exaggerated, contained at least a measure of truth (46).

The growing international popularity of reggae music no doubt played a major role in changing attitudes toward the Rastafarian movement. Previously rejected as uncultivated and crude, reggae was suddenly embraced as Jamaica's national music and one of its chief cultural exports. In a 1975 article entitled "The World Discovers Reggae," a *Gleaner* reporter summed up the expectations of many Jamaicans who now regarded reggae as Jamaica's new cultural voice: "Reggae could be the start of something really big. Something else to confirm what Jamaicans have already known—that this place we call home is one of the biggest little countries in the world" (4).

In social movement theory, the failure of "evasion," "counter-persuasion," "coercion," or "adjustment" strategies to control groups typically leads to "capitulation," or "the total acceptance of a social movement's ideology: beliefs, goals, objectives, and solutions" (Stewart, Smith, and Denton 156). Something quite different happened in Jamaica between 1972 and 1980. In response to the growing popularity of reggae, Rastafarian symbols increasingly became integrated into mainstream Jamaican society. In addition, the Rastafarians played a significant role in promoting black pride and rehabilitating Jamaica's African heritage. While the international popularity of reggae apparently enhanced the Rastafarians' cultural identity in Jamaica, much of that legitimacy was illusory. Jamaica's neo-colonial power structure remained essentially unchanged. Furthermore, the Rastafarian movement failed to achieve many of its specific policy goals, including the legalization of marijuana and repatriation to Africa. In short, the Jamaican ruling class did not capitulate to the demands of the Rastafarian movement. Instead, it tried to co-opt the cultural symbols of Rastafari and reggae music as authentic

reflections of Jamaican society. The successful co-optation of Rastafari signaled the movement's transition from an internal threat to one of
Jamaica's best-known tourist attractions.

THE RHETORIC OF CO-OPTATION

Many of the apparent concessions of the Jamaican establishment to the
growing popularity of reggae music in the 1970s might be viewed as exam-
ples of a strategy of "control" that Stewart, Smith, and Denton have labeled
"adjustment." The adjustment strategy "involves making some concessions
to a social movement while not accepting the movement's demands or
goals." Adjustment tactics can encompass "symbolic" concessions, such as
Manley's public praise of the Rastafarian movement, or establishments
might sacrifice some of their own personnel if a "social movement focuses
its agitation and hatred upon a single individual or unit" (155). If a social
movement's agitation becomes especially intense, the establishment might
even incorporate movement leaders and sympathizers into the establishment by appointing them to "non-threatening positions" (Stewart, Smith,
and Denton 156). Or the establishment might incorporate parts of the dissent ideology into the mainstream, entering into a more or less "merger"
with the social movement (Bowers, Ochs, and Jensen 63).

Yet as Stewart, Smith, and Denton have observed, "cooperation"
with a dissent group "may lead to outright *co-optation* of the cause," or a
literal takeover of the movement by elements of the mainstream establishment (156). When one considers all the "adjustments" made by the
Jamaican political and cultural establishment, as well as the significance
of some of those supposed "adjustments," one can argue that the
Jamaican ruling class did indeed "co-opt" the Rastafarian movement,
embracing its symbolism while deflecting its most substantive religious
and political "doctrines." This is not to say that Jamaican politicians,
journalists, educators, and mainstream musicians all conspired to co-opt
the movement, nor is it to say that the co-optation was ever complete.
It is to say, however, that even after Jamaica apparently embraced Rasta-

fari as a "cultural treasure," many Rastafarians remained trapped at the bottom of a neo-colonial social structure, and that most of their religious and political demands were rejected.

It was during the 1972 national campaign that PNP candidate Michael Manley portended the eventual co-optation of reggae music and the Rasta-farian movement. More than any other Jamaican politician, Manley under-stood that the exploitation of reggae music was an effective method of iden-tifying with Jamaica's younger voters and dissident groups. Sociologist Anita M. Waters, in *Race, Class, and Political Symbols: Rastafari and Reggae in Jamaican Politics*, noted the 1972 national campaign was distinguished by the "systematic and deliberate use of reggae music" (137). This tactic of inviting reggae musicians to participate in political rallies might be seen as an example of incorporating personnel into "institutional bodies" (Stewart, Smith, and Denton 156).

Thus, the PNP in 1971 hired reggae musician Clancy Eccles to write what would become one of the PNP's most heralded campaign songs, "Power for the People" (Waters 131, 133). With Eccles at the helm, the PNP sponsored a weekly musical political bandwagon. Traveling from the urban center of Kingston to the island's rural areas, the bandwagon featured eight of the top twenty-five reggae musicians of 1971 (Waters 131). Excit-ed by the prospect of mass exposure, reggae stars enthusiastically performed songs earlier banned by the JLP.

Even after Manley was elected as Jamaica's new prime minister, he con-tinued to sponsor and promote reggae music. In a 1973 interview with the *Jamaica Journal*, Manley still praised reggae music despite the music's grow-ing criticism of his economic policies:

> There are all sorts of songs that are directed against my Government, or directed against things for which my Government—as you call it—is blamed. If you take, for instance, you know . . . the problem of the cost of living; with this terrible world inflation—in which the whole world, natu-rally including Jamaica, is caught—there have been lots of songs protesting against that. And I think that's entirely healthy. . . . if anybody is going to protest against me, at least I want them to do it with style. (Manley, "A Politician" 43)

During the same interview, Manley suggested that music conservatories should open their doors to tutor reggae musicians (43). Manley even wrote an introduction to the book *Reggae International,* underscoring reggae's "musical pulse" of "survival" ("Reggae" 11). Despite Bob Marley's warning in "Revolution" (*Natty Dread*) to "never make a politician grant you a favor," Manley and the reggae star became friends. Manley often visited the reggae star at his home on Hope Road in Kingston (T. White 264).

Dudley Thompson, Manley's minister of foreign affairs from 1976 to 1977, summarized why Jamaican politicians became increasingly interested in exploiting reggae music for political ends:

> I think the politicians used reggae. Reggae, especially through people like Bob Marley, expressed the wishes and the sentiments of the people. That protest came through music and through their song. And they said what they disagreed with and agreed with. And so you can find out really how the people were thinking by what songs they sang. It was one way by which you could gage the people. (*Bob Marley: Rebel Music*)

During his two terms in office, Manley also seemed to pursue a second adjustment tactic: incorporating part of the dissent ideology. In particular, Manley sympathized publicly with the Rastafarian movement's long-standing goal of reviving Jamaica's African heritage. In a 1973 interview with the *Jamaica Journal,* Manley urged Jamaicans to "become at-ease with all the strands of its heritage." While denying he was "hung up" on Africa, Manley understood that Africa was a "clearly important aspect of development [for Jamaica]" (44). A decade later, Manley continued to emphasize the importance of recapturing Jamaica's African roots: "We were convinced that it was only through the rediscovery of our heritage that we would evolve a culture that reflected the best in ourselves because it expressed pride in what we were and where we came from" (*Jamaica* 39).

While recalling Jamaica's African roots, Manley pledged to restructure Jamaica's system of social stratification. In his first book, *The Politics of Change,* published in 1974, Manley promised to change the "imbalances" of Jamaican society where "people with light complexions enjoy[ed] a psychological advantage and consciously or unconsciously have assumed an additional 'weight' in the society" (57). The Manley government, according to political scientist Anthony Payne in *Politics in Jamaica,* tried to build its political base on a "national identity which genuinely crosses racial boundaries" (6).

The Manley government and the Rastafarians also discovered common ground, at least rhetorically, in denouncing the wide gap between wealth and poverty in Jamaica. Manley surmised that democratic socialism could best address the multiplying problems of unemployment, inadequate housing, and crime. He believed a new government in Jamaica should "dismantle the apparatus of privilege" (*The Politics* 37). Manley sponsored numerous social programs in Jamaica, from the Special Employment Programme (SEP), which employed poor Jamaicans in sanitation jobs, to Operation GROW, a program to help boost Jamaica's agricultural sector (Panton 43–4). At first, at least, democratic socialism appealed to the Rastafarians' sense of economic justice. As Callam put it: "Rastas discovered they had something in common with the proponents of the democratic socialist philosophy" (42).

Manley employed a third adjustment tactic in agreeing to hold public meetings with Rastafarian "leaders" and groups. In 1973, Manley met with members of a Rastafarian group, the Jah Rastafari Hola Coptic Church, to examine the movement's demand for land reform in Jamaica. During the meeting, Manley offered the group several thousand acres of land. According to Barry Chevannes, Manley wanted unemployed ghetto youths, who had come to identify with the Rastafarian movement, to become interested in agriculture. Manley believed if ghetto youths became involved in farming, they would be less likely to turn to crime (Chevannes, *Rastafari* 193). Other Rastafarian groups chided the Hola Coptic Church for "'selling out'" to the government, and the Hola Coptic Church ultimately rejected Manley's offer because it would have seemed "contrary to the interest of the movement" relative to repatriation (Chevannes, *Rastafari* 194). Nevertheless, Manley's willingness to meet with Rastafarian groups and to discuss their demands marked an important break from the past.

In March 1976, Manley met with another Rastafarian group, the Centralizing Committee of the Rastafarian Selassie I Divine Theocratic

Government, to discuss the problem of police harassment ("Rastas Meet" 9). Three months prior to the meeting, Manley told the *Gleaner* that it was "wrong" for security forces to persecute those wearing dreadlocks. In the article, Manley was reported as saying that "the fact that a man has locks does not make him a wrong-doer" ("PM Says" 15). During the March meeting, according to the *Gleaner*, Manley expressed his desire to solve the problem of police intimidation, announcing that the PNP had "completely accepted the rights of the Rasta Brethren to the practices of their religion particularly refering to their style of dress and their dreadlocks" ("Rastas Meet" 9). Although some Rastafarian spokespersons complained three months after the meeting that Manley had not adequately responded to the issue ("Rastafarians Seek" 2), police harassment of the Rastafarians reportedly decreased by the mid- to late 1970s (Miles 5).

The growing international popularity of reggae undoubtedly played a crucial role in bringing about these "adjustments" in the official attitudes toward Rastafari. In a 1990 article, Chevannes recalled how Jamaica's colonial ruler, Great Britain, historically had downplayed Jamaica's African heritage and glorified Europe as the beacon of civilization. European cultures had been promoted in Jamaica as more pure, handsome, moral, and civilized than black or African cultures (Chevannes, "Healing" 62–6). Even after independence, the JLP continued to reify themes of European superiority, dismissing Rastafari and reggae as "crude" throwbacks to a "dark" and "silent" Africa.

As the international community increasingly embraced reggae music as an important cultural form, however, middle-class criticism of reggae and Rastafari in Jamaica was "silenced" (Chevannes, "Healing" 79). Rather than viewing reggae music as a pathological response by Jamaica's dispossessed classes, the Jamaican government and many of its supporters co-opted this dissident cultural form as something positive and distinctively "Jamaican."

Reflecting Manley's sympathy for the Rastafarians and the success of "international" reggae music, even the *Daily Gleaner*, which had long dismissed reggae as "primitive" and "unsophisticated," changed its tune. In the 1970s, the *Gleaner* printed information about new reggae releases, interviewed reggae stars, and provided information concerning local and international reggae tours ("Merry," 1975 4–5; Tafari 4). The *Gleaner* and other Jamaican newspapers and magazines were especially eager to follow the career of Jamaica's leading reggae band, Bob Marley and the Wailers. The *Gleaner* printed articles with headlines such as "Bob Marley the 'Prophet'" and "Golden Year Likely for Bob Marley and the Wailers." Dermot Hussey's "Bob Marley, The Man of Music for 1975," was one of the first articles to predict Marley's ascent as the first "third-world" superstar. Marley was the new international ambassador of Jamaican culture.

The *Gleaner* also changed its tune regarding the Rastafarian movement. In the 1960s, the *Gleaner* characterized the Rastafarians as "violent revolutionaries," but in the 1970s the paper often supported, even celebrated the movement. In a 1976 article, "Ganja Revolution," for example, the *Gleaner* expressed sympathy for the Rastafarian cause and conceded that the Rastafarians were correct about the destructive effects of "Babylon" (3). The *Gleaner* interviewed "Rockers," a Rastafarian youth, about his Rastafarian beliefs ("A Rasta Youth" 8). The *Gleaner* also printed letters testifying to the Jamaican public's new respect for the movement. In one letter, Howard Brown claimed that the Rastafarians "can feel a special pride in the fact that they were pioneers in Jamaica, if not throughout the world" (17). In a letter entitled "Rastas and Contributions to Our Society," Aderemi Atai celebrated the movement's new legitimacy after years of struggle against discrimination and prejudice (7).

The *Gleaner* even hired Rastafarian journalists, including Dennis Forsythe and Arthur Kitchin. Forsythe's writings, such as the 1979 article entitled "Rastas and the African Lion," often celebrated the Rastafarians' African heritage. Kitchin's editorials explored a variety of Rastafarian issues, from the pseudo-Rastafarian group, the Ethiopian Zion Coptic Church, to questions about the movement's future in Jamaica. Reflecting on the movement's growing political influence, Kitchin did caution the Rastafarians, however, to recognize the "obvious trap" of political manipulation ("Rastas" 6).

Other mainstream institutions of Jamaican society also began to appropriate Rastafarian symbols and reggae music as "its own" in the 1970s. Jamaica's theatre companies began to produce plays showcasing Rastafarian themes and reggae music. In 1976, two plays, "Summer Dread" and "I-Man" played to Jamaican audiences (Waters 177). In a review of the 1978 play "Explaintations," *Gleaner* columnist Dawn Ritch expressed a "swelling of emotional pride" during a performance by one of Jamaica's most popular reggae bands, Third World. Ritch declared that "reggae music has rarely been raised to such levels of joyous exhilaration" ("Something" 6). In 1980, a *Gleaner* reporter, writing under the pseudonym "Showman," proclaimed it a historic day as "Reggae," a show featuring reggae music, opened on Broadway (4).

Rather than condemning reggae music as an incitement to violence, politicians apparently had come to view reggae music as a force of unity and peace in Jamaica. In 1978, Bob Marley headlined the One Love Peace Concert, a festival created to bring political peace to Jamaica. Organized by Bucky Marshall (PNP) and Claudie Massop (JLP)—two gang leaders who unofficially affiliated themselves with Jamaica's two mainstream political parties— the One Love Peace Concert was attended and praised by the leaders of Jamaica's two political parties. According to the *Gleaner*, Manley and JLP leader Edward Seaga danced a "short jig" at the concert ("PM, Seaga" 1). While generally not known for expressing sympathy for either the Rastafarian movement or reggae music, Seaga even applauded reggae's "peacemaking" potential. In a 1978 article headlined, "Seaga Thanks Marley," Seaga praised Marley's performance at the concert and assured the reggae star that the concert would promote the efforts to support the "Campaign for Peace" (2).

Reggae Sunsplash, an annual tourist festival created in 1978, is perhaps the clearest example of how the Jamaican government and its surrogates tried to co-opt the Rastafarian movement. Unlike the One Love concert, Reggae Sunsplash was officially sponsored by the Jamaican government. This tourist event has lured thousands of international visitors to Jamaica to listen to some of Jamaica's top reggae artists. Reggae Sunsplash has become an economic boon to a country increasingly dependent on tourism as its main foreign-exchange earner. As a highly popular and profitable tourist event, Reggae Sunsplash has even been duplicated in the United States and Japan (Chevannes, *Rastafari* 272).

In effect, these "adjustments" did bring about important changes in racial attitudes of most Jamaicans. Before the popularity of reggae music and the Rastafarian movement, many Jamaicans—especially the ruling classes—believed that "Blackness" was akin to "impurity" and "evil" (Chevannes, "Healing" 62). In her study on the Rastafarian movement and Jamaican politics, Anita M. Waters interviewed a respondent, a 1976 JLP political candidate, who had this to say about the Rastafarians' influence on trans-forming the meaning of "black" as a racial category: "I respect the Rasta thing. They have a very proud, positive attitude toward blackness." In that same study, another respondent observed that the "Rastas sensitised the national consciousness in attitudes toward black and poor" (qtd. in Waters 176). Cultural critic Stuart Hall has remarked the Rastafarians were instru-mental in rearticulating "blackness" from a negative to a positive sign (107–13). Recent empirical studies also have confirmed that by the early 1980s there was a dramatic, positive change in Jamaican attitudes toward "black" as a racial category (Richardson 158). As a result, Chevannes claimed the Rastafarians had performed an "exorcism" in an attempt to eradicate racism in Jamaica ("Healing" 59). In this way, the Rastafarians gained a cultural identity as all Jamaicans came to view "black" as a more positive racial category.

In much the same way, the Rastafarian movement changed Jamaican's attitudes about Africa. Although Jamaica's lower classes idealized Africa as their historical and spiritual homeland, the middle to upper classes often dismissed Africa as the "silent" and "dark" continent. In a 1994 interview, Chevannes observed that Jamaica's middle class "saw their role as one of assimilation and assimilating the cultural values of the colonial ruling class." By the late 1970s, however middle-class Jamaicans were more inclined to "identify more with the African reference point than with the European" ("Healing" 79). Rastafarian scholar Leahcim T. Semaj main-tained that Rastafari played a pivotal role in changing a society dominated by European ideals to one where "there is now hope for Black self-determi-nation" ("Race and Identity" 18). The Rastafarians were successful in encouraging the upper classes to reexamine their African identity.

At first glance, all of these changes appeared to grant the Rastafarians a "victory" in Jamaica. Yet considered all together, these "adjustments" also can be seen as co-optation of the cultural symbols of Rastafari without "capitulation" to the movement's specific policy demands—much as some pseudo-Rastafarian groups embraced the movement's symbols and fashion while rejecting its religious practices or political doctrines and goals. Writing for the now-defunct *Jamaican Daily News*, journalist Trevor Fearon sensed this possibility as he questioned the sincerity of those Jamaicans who once dismissed reggae but were now "suddenly speaking about them [reggae artists] as their long-time brethren" (21). As we consider the response of the Manley government and its supporters to some of the Rastafarians' more substantive political, economic, and religious demands, we shall see that Fearon's suspicions were indeed well founded. While the Rastafarians' cultural identity was legitimized in Jamaica, the movement achieved few of its policy goals.

THE ILLUSION OF VICTORY

Anthropologist Leonard Barrett has maintained that the Rastafarians, as a partial result of international reggae's popularity, achieved what rhetorical scholars commonly refer to as "legitimacy" (146). Legitimacy is the "right" to "exercise authority" (Francesconi 49). Groups with "legitimacy" have the power to reward or punish less legitimate groups. Social movements strive for legitimacy (Stewart, Smith, and Denton 131). In his study of European labor movements, Gaston V. Rimlinger argued that, for social movements to be considered successful, they must secure legitimacy from several sources: "The workers' demands and their methods of enforcing them must somehow become legitimate in the eyes of the employers, the government, the public, and the workers themselves" (363).

While Jamaica's upper classes often embraced Rastafarian symbols, the movement did not achieve its specific policy goals. The Jamaican government and its supporters did not, of course, capitulate or willingly transfer political power to the Rastafarians. Instead, the Manley government publicly sympathized with the movement but made only token concessions. In fact, critics such as political scientist Klaus de Albuquerque contended that Manley and the PNP "publicly identify with the Rastafari[an] movement, while privately condemning it as a barrier to the construction of a socialist Jamaica" (46).

While the Rastafarians' cultural identity was legitimized, this victory did little to restructure the class system in Jamaica. While more Jamaicans from the black class entered the ranks of the traditional "brown" middle class, Manley stopped short of dislocating the traditional "white" and "brown" power structure in Jamaica. During this period, according to Waters, "[e]conomic power in Jamaica still reside[d] to a great extent with White and fair groups. . . . With status as well as wealth, Whites have the most and Blacks the least" (29).

The Rastafarians' new legitimacy also did little to bring economic justice for Jamaica's poor people. Many Rastafarians initially approved of Manley's economic reforms, but Jamaica's economy deteriorated significantly during the 1970s. While an international energy crisis played a pivotal role in Jamaica's rapidly shrinking economy, Manley's own economic policies, according to public policy expert David Panton, "served as the major cause of the decline in the Jamaican economy" (57). Yet whatever the cause, Jamaica's disintegrating economic base left the Rastafarians and other poor Jamaicans still trapped in the stifling ghettos of West Kingston. Before long, reggae musicians were again protesting against the government's failure to help Jamaica's poor. In 1974, for example, the Ethiopians released a song criticizing Manley, "Promises, Promises," and in that same year, Max Romeo's song, "No, Joshua, No," warned Manley that "Rasta" was "watching and blaming you" for Jamaica's economic woes (qtd. in Waters 184).

Nor did the Manley government concede to the Rastafarians' more specific demands, such as repatriation to Africa. Although Manley was rumored to have met with a Rastafarian group in 1976 to discuss the issue of repatriation (Waters 177), the PNP government never created an official plan for repatriation. Unable to secure the support of the Manley government, the Rastafarian movement attempted to create its own repatriation plan. By the 1970s, a small group of Rastafarians were living on a farming settlement in Shashamane, Ethiopia (Campbell, *Rasta* 224). However, in

1974, Haile Selassie's monarchy was overthrown, and the new military government nationalized all of Ethiopia's rural land while the "poor of Shashamane seized all the tractors, land and assets" of the small Rastafarian community. Eventually, the new government returned a small plot of land to the Rastafarians who "wanted to stay" (Campbell, *Rasta* 226), but the failure of the Shashamane experiment demonstrated the Rastafarians' inability to successfully repatriate its own followers to Africa.

Manley also refused to recognize the religious significance of ganja, or marijuana, to the Rastafarians. During his first term in office, Manley promised the Rastafarians he would review Jamaica's marijuana laws (Yawney 235) and grant pardons to those serving long-term prison terms for marijuana possession. Yet for the remainder of his time in office, he supported only minor reductions in the penalties for marijuana possession in Jamaica.[2] Manley even cooperated with the U.S. government's efforts to eradicate Jamaica's marijuana trade (Campbell, *Rasta* 112). In 1973, for example, President Richard Nixon launched an anti-drug operation called "Operation Buccaneer," which included "search and destroy" missions aimed at Jamaica's marijuana fields (Campbell, *Rasta* 112–14). Manley cooperated fully in this effort, apparently convinced that the ganja trade needed to be controlled in order to achieve political stability in Jamaica. Critics claim that Manley's support for Operation Buccaneer was a heavy-handed effort to suppress the Rastafarian movement (Campbell, *Rasta* 114). At the 1978 One Love Peace Concert in Jamaica, reggae star Peter Tosh even went as far publicly to "lecture Michael Manley and [JLP leader] Edward Seaga for their failure to support the legalization of ganja" (T. White 301). During the concert, Tosh also attacked Jamaica's corrupt social and political system:

> I and I have to set up this country and eliminate all those shitstem [system] that black poor people don't live in confusion cause hunger people are angry people. If the government just come together and say right now if you want to build this country and build the people, 'cause right now can't build the country and don't build the people. People suffering from malnutrition and all them thing there. Is just a shitstem that laid down to belittle the poor. You no seen? (*Stepping Razor*)

Meanwhile, Jamaica's radio stations continued to marginalize reggae music as a form of political discourse.3 Although Jamaica's radio stations seemed to make concessions to the popularity of international reggae by adding more indigenous music to their playlists, they still played reggae music during the less desirable time slots in the middle of the night. In the mid-1970s, one of Jamaica's two national radio stations, Radio Jamaica Rediffusion, adopted a policy of playing 50 percent reggae and 50 percent foreign music ("Merry," 1976, 4). Yet a *Daily Gleaner* entertainment columnist remarked: "Guess when they play most reggae music? Between 1:00 a.m. and 5:00 a.m., when the vast majority of the people are sleeping" ("Merry Go" 1976, 4). Mickey Dread hosted a program, "Dread at the Controls," from midnight until 4:30 in the morning. Dread explained why Jamaica's radio stations were still reluctant to play reggae music: "They were old-fashioned, you know. Jamaica Broadcasting Corporation, I mean they've got help from the British to set up this radio station, so, normally, they followed what they were told to do from their parents, right, instead of actually catering for the local community" (qtd. in Gordon C 80).

Even with its new international popularity, reggae was thus "facing a lot of barriers" in Jamaica, as *Gleaner* columnist Hugh Bembridge observed ("Reggae Artists" 8). On August 14, 1976, a *Daily Gleaner* entertainment columnist wrote a scathing editorial in the paper's entertainment column, "Merry Go Round," criticizing the lack of airtime for reggae as an "unpatriotic" policy. "[I]t is stupid and very unpatriotic for the island's leading radio station [RJR] to be defending a policy of 50% reggae and 50% rhythm and blues," the writer argued, "when it is quite aware that the masses, the vast majority of the people, are consistently pro-reggae" (4).

Jamaican radio stations also continued to ban outright certain "controversial" reggae songs. In 1975, Jamaica's radio stations banned three of Peter Tosh's songs, including the pro-ganja song "Legalize It" (T. White 269). Unlike the JLP's hard-line tactics to censor reggae music, Manley claimed not to favor the banning of "Legalize It" and wrote Tosh to express his disappointment over the decision (de Albuquerque, "The Future" 44). Tosh, however, was not appeased:

> The radio stations is [sic] a pack of shit and I hate it badly for that. It is
> trying to defamate the character of reggae music and make those who are
> playing reggae music look like fools. When I go to other places, I am treated
> like a king. In the place where reggae music is originated, the people who
> make reggae music are treated like dogs. (qtd. in Salaam 114)

In short, while the Rastafarians' cultural identity was legitimized in
Jamaica in the 1970s, this did little to improve their political and economic status in Jamaica or to help them realize their more specific policy goals.
Jamaica remained a racially stratified society, and most Rastafarians continued to live in poverty in crowded slums and shantytowns. The government
continued to resist efforts at repatriation to Africa, and it even stepped up
efforts to control an important element in the Rastafarian religion: the
smoking of ganja. Even as reggae achieved international popularity, the
music remained marginalized on Jamaica's own radio stations, especially the
more political controversial songs.

Perhaps learning from the JLP's failure to suppress the Rastafarian
movement, Michael Manley employed more "adjustment" tactics in
responding to the growing international popularity of reggae and the
attention it brought to the Rastafarians and Jamaica itself. Manley invited reggae musicians to play at political rallies and forged a link between
Rastafari and the political philosophy of democratic socialism. Many of
Manley's supporters began to embrace Rastafari and reggae music as
something distinctly "Jamaican." The *Daily Gleaner* published articles
praising reggae's positive contributions to Jamaica's society. From the
theatre to tourism, Jamaican society seemed to embrace Rastafari and
reggae music.

Although the Manley government may have embraced many of the
Rastafarian movement's most important cultural symbols, this did little to
change the political and economic status of Rastafarians in Jamaica. The
Rastafarians remained second-class citizens in Jamaica's racially stratified
social structure. In short, the Manley government co-opted the movement,
transforming a political threat into one of Jamaica's best-known cultural
attractions and an economic asset.

This co-optation of the Rastafarians may have played a significant role in the decline of the movement in the 1980s. As the *Daily Gleaner* reported, the Rastafarian movement appeared "in eclipse" by the late 1980s (E. Henry 8). The *Gleaner* speculated that the movement's decline was related to the rise of both Rastafarian intellectuals (Kitchin, "Rastafari Movement" 8), and secular middle-class Rastafarian groups (Boyne 23), as well as the movement's failure to unify its various groups (Kitchin, "Defining" 8, 13). The Jamaican youth also became decidedly less interested in reggae, preferring instead new genres of Jamaican music called "dancehall," "digital," and "ragga."

From the perspective of the Jamaican establishment, then, the strategy of co-optation appeared to have been successful. The next logical step in co-optation was to transform reggae and Rastafari into tourist attractions and Jamaica's chief exports.

EPILOGUE

[S]o important has reggae proven to our economy that it is seen as a major foreign exchange earner as well as a major promotional entity for industry, particular tourism. . . . Indeed, Reggae is to Jamaica what boxing is to the United States—national economic benefit, promotion and the improvement of the lot of many poor and impoverished youths.

—Eron Henry

During the 1970s, the Jamaican establishment and its surrogates employed an adjustment tactic, co-optation, to transform reggae music and the Rastafarians into what some have considered a "cultural fad." In recent years, Rastafarian images and reggae music have become increasingly important in the promotion of Jamaica's tourist industry. Many Caribbean and Pacific Basin islands have restructured their economics away from relying on agricultural exports (de Albuquerque and McElroy 619). As a result, many of these countries, including Jamaica, have turned to tourism as the primary foreign-exchange earner. With raked sandy white beaches and brilliant, crystal blue waters, Jamaica is a natural setting for tourists to experience the four S's of tourism: sand, sea, surf, and sex.

From pamphlets to television commercials, Jamaica conspicuously markets reggae and the symbols of Rastafari as part of its rich cultural heritage. In a wide range of promotional materials, models clad in the symbols of Rastafari (e.g., dreadlocks, Rasta colors) are portrayed as eager and happy participants, willing to help fulfill a tourist's "fantasy vacation." In much the same way, travel brochures highlight reggae's "happy" and "peaceful" themes, while obscuring the music's lyrics of social rage. The rise of a new breed of pseudo-Rastafarians, commonly referred to as Rent-a-Dreads, further accentuates the connection between the movement and tourism.

Yet, the co-optation of reggae music and the Rastafarian movement were never complete or entirely successful. By the mid-1990s, reggae music was making a comeback of sorts in Jamaica during what could almost be called a "civil war" between local gangs and the Jamaican State and civilian population. Reacting to the high murder rate and the downward turn in the economy, Jamaican musicians relied more and more on the protest messages of Rastafari: messages of social rage and spiritual hope. These messages, of course, contradicted the Jamaican tourist industry's image of Jamaica: an idyllic paradise in the sun.

REGGAE, RASTAFARI, AND TOURISM
Development of Tourism in Jamaica

Shortly after World War II, the international tourist industry boomed. From 1950 to 1982, the number of tourists traveling worldwide increased from an estimated 25 million in 1950 to 300 million in 1982 (Conway 2). More recently, as reported in the *Commercial Appeal*, experts estimated that international tourists numbered 612 million worldwide in 1997, and will increase to 1.6 billion by 2020 (Shea, screen 1).

Jamaica was one of the first Caribbean countries to benefit from the tourism boom because of its comparatively well-developed hotel and airport facilities, and because of its economic ties to developed countries such as the United States and Great Britain (Conway 2). Since the 1960s, foreign investors have largely controlled Jamaica's tourist industry. According to urban geographer Dennis Conway, international tourism benefits a number of private enterprises, from travel agents to advertising agencies to tour operators (2). Paralleling the limited role of most Caribbean governments in the development of their tourist industries, Jamaica enticed foreign businesses to invest in tourism through "fiscal incentives, infrastructure and utilities, and modestly financed promotional activities" (Conway 7).

In the late 1950s, with its temperate climate and natural beauty, Jamaica was originally marketed as a new island "paradise." By promoting Jamaica as "paradise," the tourism industry was selling Jamaica as a type of "touristic culture." As Rex Nettleford explained, "[V]isitors do not normally come, and are not encouraged to come to the region to 'soak up' its culture. The marketing strategies have themselves been soaked in something called 'Paradise.'"

Since the mid-1960s, many Caribbean nations have also promoted "cultural tourism" (commonly referred to as "heritage tourism"). According to Nettleford, cultural tourism lured "visitors to their monuments, sites and ruins or to anything else that is marketable as a distinctive cultural attribute." Cultural artifacts may include stories, dance, or religious expressions. According to Nettleford, Jamaica has been lucky in its own efforts because cultural tourism came only after notions of a "cultural policy for the building of Jamaican nationhood and identity were well established" ("Heritage" 8).

The Jamaican government, the Jamaica Tourist Board (JTB), and local entrepreneurs played an important role in promoting reggae and the images of Rastafari as Jamaica's chief cultural attractions. Foreign investors and the Jamaican government recognized that many international travelers associate Jamaica primarily with two things: reggae and, to a lesser extent, Rastafari. Despite a brief decline in tourism during the mid-1970s, the two marketing strategies—touristic culture and cultural tourism—have been extremely successful in attracting tourists to the island nation. Jamaica's tourist industry has continued to prosper into the 1990s. By the early 1990s, tourism was the nation's leading foreign-exchange earner, growing at an annual rate of 7 percent per year (Luntta 37).

Tourism Promotion of Reggae and Rastafari

Reggae Sunsplash in 1978 epitomized the new "partnership" of the Jamaican government, Jamaica's tourism industry, the Rastafarian move- ment, and reggae music. In 1978, four black Jamaicans (through their Syn- ergy Productions Limited) created Sunsplash to "promote both the music and the island's scenic appeal" (George and Fergusson 62). The resort town of Montego Bay hosted the first Reggae Sunsplash, a week-long musical fes- tival featuring Jamaica's best-known reggae stars and celebrating the music's contribution to Jamaican culture. Sunsplash received partial sponsorship through a governmental agency, the Jamaica Tourist Board. Since 1993, a new reggae festival, Reggae Sumfest, has competed with Sunsplash for tal- ent, tourists, and money.[1]

Typically an annual event, Reggae Sunsplash and Sumfest are center- pieces of Jamaica's tourist promotions. Thousands now visit Jamaica to experience not only its warm climate and sandy beaches, but also the allur- ing sound of reggae and the mysterious "cult" of Rastafari. Nettleford has argued that Reggae Sunsplash "attracts certain visitors . . . to share in the heritage of popular music which is the creation of the people of Jamaica and now deemed as natural to it as are the sun, the sand and the sea" ("Heritage" 9).

After Bob Marley's death from cancer in 1981, even the memory of the reggae star became something of a tourist attraction. Marley's house in Kingston became the "Bob Marley Museum," complete with a gift shop and a restaurant serving traditional "I-tal" Rastafarian foods and juices. Tourists are escorted through Marley's herbal garden, view a room wallpapered with over two hundred magazine and newspaper articles covering the career of the Wailers, and watch a twenty-minute biographical film on Marley's life and career. In Trenchtown, a poor suburb in West Kingston where Marley began singing with the Wailers in the early 1960s, residents and fans of the reggae star are transforming a few rundown buildings into a new Bob Marley museum (Rosenberg, "Bob Marley's" A2). Across the island, the Bob Marley Mausoleum (again with a gift shop) has been erected in the singer's birthplace, Nine Miles, located in the parish of St. Ann. Jamaica has designated Marley's birthday as a national holiday, commemorated with the Bob Marley Birthday Bash, an annual four-day musical festival celebrating the life of the reggae star (Luntta 61). Tourists from around the world flock to this and other festivals celebrating Marley and the music he made famous.

Yet the exploitation of reggae music and Rastafarian imagery in promoting Jamaican tourism has gone well beyond invoking the memory of Bob Marley. In all sorts of promotional materials, the enchanting sounds of reggae and the image of the smiling "Rastaman" beckoned tourists from around the world to Jamaica's major tourist areas. The tourist guide *Caribbean for Lovers*, for example, touts the "sensual beat" of reggae music and the "cult" of Rastafari, while other guides—*Frommer's Jamaica and Barbados*, *Fodor's Exploring Caribbean*, and *Jamaica Handbook*—provide brief histories of the movement and discuss the international popularity of reggae music.[2] In the travel guide *Access Caribbean*, tourists are encouraged to dance to the "rhythms of a reggae band" and "adopt the Jamaicans' unofficial motto: 'Don't Worry, Be Happy'" (Dempsey and Karle 162). Writing for another tourist guide, *Berlitz Travellers Guide to the Caribbean*, travel writer Jennifer Quale observed: "[T]he best reason to go to Jamaica is to be captivated by the seductive rhythms that keep the rest of the world at bay" (36). Similarly, *Fodor's 92: Jamaica* opens with the image of a "grinning" Rastafarian watching a blonde female MBA student, a New York lawyer, and a honeymooning couple sway "to a joyous reggae beat drifting across a splendid expanse of white, powdery sand." All "celebrate" the "sweet life" of Jamaica because "whatever you ask, the answer is the same. . . . [n]o problem, *mon*" (Diedrichs 1).

Many brochures which feature a rainbow of Jamaican resorts and hotels (from five star to economy) play up reggae and Bob Marley. The *Adventure Tours USA Sun Escapes* catalogue mentions in the "Tours Available" section, the "Kingston Bob Marley Tour" (42). The *Jamaica-Jamaica* brochure in the night entertainment section mentions "[t]he rich reggae music which Jamaica has given the world will soak into your very bones; . . . kick off your shoes and your inhibitions to dance to a primordial rhythm at our beach party" (14). In another example, the *Negril Jamaica: Into the '90s!* brochure describes Negril as a place where one can hear the "intoxicating sounds of the famous Reggae beat" (1).

Beyond travel guides and brochures, magazines such as *Modern Bride, National Geographic Traveler,* and *Road and Track* use reggae as a metaphor for describing "paradise." In a *Modern Bride* article entitled "Jamaica— Romance to the Reggae Beat," the authors blend the "sound" of reggae with images of paradise: "Like the easygoing yet stirring syncopation of the reggae music that was born here, Jamaica's landscape is at once startling and soothing in its beauty" (Bain 364). Throughout the article, the musical phrase "rhythm" attempts to capture the emotional experience of visiting Jamaica. Tourists move to "joyous rhythms of this island paradise" and slip "into the 'soon come' rhythm of island time" (Bain 440, 434). In another example, a *National Geographic Traveler* reporter weaves "Rastafari" and "reggae" into a seamless, exotic narrative:

> A motorboat zoomed past my patch of sand, towing the billowing green and black umbrella of a parasail. . . . A *dreadlocked*, megaphone-toting tout strolled by, exhorting us all to attend the big show that night at De Buss restaurant. . . . While I couldn't quite catch the words of the *reggae songs* that were rolling across the sand, they were beginning to strike me as unerringly true and vitally important [emphasis mine].(Martin 104)

Of course, travel guides and magazines extensively utilize information provided by tourism boards as well as convention and visitors bureaus, both of which are typically supported either partially or totally by governmental funding.

Ironically, the JTB only recently incorporated reggae and Rastafarian images in their promotional materials. According to a 1991 article entitled "Reggae's Growth in the '90s," the JTB "used Reggae music for the first time and won several awards for their advertisement on Jamaica" (Harris 5C). In

a 1994 interview, Dermot Hussey discussed the JTB's reluctance to promote
Jamaica's cultural heritage:

> [After the popularity of reggae in the 1970s] it took them [the JTB] at
> least 20 odd years to do that [include reggae and Rastafarian images into
> JTB promotional materials] because before the Tourist Board would have
> never done that. And they just did that in the eighties, you know. . . . you
> even see a dreadlock in a commercial now with a baby—a white kid—that
> would have been totally taboo. . . . You just have to go back and look at the
> ads that are there from the tourist board and you'll see [the absence of reg-
> gae and Rastafarian images].

In a JTB brochure entitled "Jamaica," Rastafarian images and reggae music
are clearly represented as an important part of Jamaica's "cultural heritage."
The document intersects brief descriptions of Jamaica's historical roots and
tourist resorts with pictures of romance dinners, golf courses, waterfalls, and
old historical buildings. The brochure includes a picture of an older, smiling
Jamaican (presumably a Rastafarian) who sports a hat with Rastafarian colors:
red, green, and gold. The brochure also includes a full color page photo of a
reggae band in concert (18). A recent JTB advertisement in *Currents*, the
magazine for Carnival Cruiseline guests, features photos of a large Rastaman
wooden carving as well as a street vendor displaying caps featuring the Rastafarian colors (Jamaica 5). Television commercials sponsored by the JTB and
the Jamaican Convention and Visitors Bureau (JCVB) feature reggae music
and Rastafarian imagery (e.g., dreadlocks, Rasta colors) urging the viewer to
call 1-800-4REGGAE for a free information package.

Because Rastafarian symbols have become an intimate part of Jamaica's
mainstream culture, one cannot know for certain whether the individuals
photographed (sporting Rasta colors and dreadlocks) are actual members of
the movement. However, governmental agencies such as the JTB have
made a conscious decision to highlight the movement's symbols in its promotional literature, thereby deliberately accentuating the connection
between Rastafari and tourism.

Air Jamaica, Jamaica's national airline (the Jamaican government retains
25 percent ownership, the rest is owned and managed by a consortium of

Jamaican investors) in its magazine ads often use reggae and Bob Marley as a recurring theme in its promotional materials. For example, the guide encourages tourists to "come to Jamaica," and quoting a Bob Marley and the Wailers' song, "and feel all right" (*Air Jamaica* 36). Other airlines attract tourists to Jamaica with commercials blending reggae music, dreadlocked Jamaicans, and lush tropical images of an island "paradise." American Airlines, for example, use Bob Marley and the Wailers' ode to universal unity, "One Love / People Get Ready," to sell Jamaica as an oasis of peace and serenity. In the ad, the narrator intones "come visit Jamaica" as visual images of swaying palm trees, waterfalls, and sandy beaches flash on the screen. The images of an island paradise, and song's refrain—"One love / One heart / Let's get together and feel all right"—work in concert to suggest a "safe" Jamaica. The commercial closes with the camera focused on the logo: "Jamaica: One Love."

Once in Jamaica, international travelers can purchase a variety of reggae and Rastafarian souvenirs. Street vendors (called "higglers") and gift shop clerks display and sell items ranging from ganja T-shirts to fake Rastafarian dreadlocks to inexpensive posters of reggae stars. Indeed, many gift store souvenirs are decorated with the Rastafarian colors of red, green, and gold.3 Writing in the *Sunday Gleaner* in 1992, Basil Walters, a Rastafarian, remarked: "Take a casual stroll around the tourist areas, and one cannot escape the images reflecting the Rasta consciousness. T-shirts and clothing with Rastafari motifs are the most common items sold to visitors to this country" (12A).

In a wide range of promotional materials, Rastafarians are portrayed as smiling, ganja-smoking servants willing to accommodate foreign visitors. The Rastafarians are not depicted as a social movement engaged in the task of reforming Jamaica's neo-colonial society and/or returning to Africa. Moreover, travel brochures emphasize reggae's "joyous" and "peaceful" themes, while denying the music's call for revolutionary change in society. These images of the reggae "guitar-strumming" Rastaman (e.g., Bob Marley) are interwoven into a larger narrative of an island paradise. The two marketing strategies—touristic culture (e.g., paradise themes) and cultural tourism (e.g., reggae)—have been extremely successful in attracting tourists to Jamaica. And a new breed of pseudo-Rastafarians called Rent-a-Dreads have also been successful in attracting female tourists to Jamaica for romance, courtship, and sex.

The Rent-a-Dreads

Rent-a-Dreads, often called "Rentas," are part of the informal "romance tourism" industry (Pruitt and LaFont 422–40).[4] Since the 1970s, women have traveled to the four corners of the globe—from Gambia to Brazil to Jamaica—seeking out new, foreign male "escorts" (de Albuquerque, "In Search" 83). Some female tourists want to redefine confining gender roles or engage in "forbidden" interracial relationships; others simply desire a new "cultural experience" (Pruitt and LaFont 425–8).

Since the 1970s, the Rentas—young, often uneducated and unskilled Jamaican men—have locked their hair and assimilated themselves within the Rastafarian community "to appeal to women tourists" (Pruitt and LaFont 433). In these tourist zones, Rent-a-Dreads advertise their carefully constructed Rastafarian identity by shaking their dreadlocks dry on beaches (de Albuquerque, "In Search" 84). In addition, many Rentas adopt a Rastafarian dialect and create a "presentation that expresses the Rastafarian emphasis on simplicity and living in harmony with nature." For the female tourist, the Rentas seemingly possess many favorable qualities: "The penchant foreign women have for men with dreadlocks is fueled by the mystique associated with the dreadlock singers of the international reggae music culture who project an image of the Rastaman as a confident, naturally powerful, and especially virile man" (Pruitt and LaFont 431).

This relationship is often built on a strict social-exchange "contract." While female tourists attempt to fulfill a "fantasy" vacation, Rentas "view a relationship with a foreign woman as a meaningful opportunity for them to capture the love and money they desire" (Pruitt and LaFont 428). A female tourist will often supply her Rent-a-Dread with free drinks and meals, access to night entertainment, and a small cash allowance (de

Albuquerque, "In Search" 84). According to political scientist Klaus de Albuquerque, African American women are "known for their interest in long-term relationships with Jamaican men," representing for many Rentas the "best chance to obtain a highly coveted U.S. green card" ("In Search" 84–5).

Predictably, many Rentas attend two of Jamaica's most popular festivals, Reggae Sunsplash and Reggae Sumfest. In the January 20, 1988, edition of the *Daily Gleaner,* reporter Suzanne Dodds characterized the Rentas as a loose confederation of male gigolos: "The Rentas, whether in booths or out, will place themselves in positions of availability. Female tourists looking to purchase will browse about so as to make the best selection. A few Prime Rentas may not reach The Splash until the last weekend, but most go on sale as early as two days before commencement" (6).

Despite the economic advantages, Rentas are often shunned by Rastafarian communities. The Rentas' desire for easy money and material gain is in direct opposition to authentic Rastafarians who "repudiates material accumulation and participation in the system of exploitative lifestyles" (Pruitt and LaFont 433). As expected, Rentas are rejected by the wider Jamaican society for "dealing with foreigners" (Pruitt and LaFont 432).

Without a doubt, the international tourist industry, the Jamaican government, and the Jamaica Tourist Board have consciously marketed Rastafarian symbols and reggae music as part of Jamaica's cultural heritage. The Rent-a-Dreads represent the ever-increasing fragmentation of the movement and symbolize efforts to identify Rastafari with tourism. In addition, Rent-a-Dreads have co-opted Rastafarian symbols—dreadlocks, the lingo, ganja—as a means to maximize their desirability as profit-seeking participants in Jamaica's romance tourism industry. While reggae and Rastafari images have become successful marketing tools, reggae music—at least—is currently regaining its popularity in Jamaica, partly in response to the ever-growing cycle of violence that has plagued the island-nation in recent years.

Epilogue

THE OTHER SIDE OF JAMAICA: GANG
WARFARE AND VIOLENCE

Reviewing Jamaica's past and uncertain future, one observer noted that
violence in Jamaican society was by all accounts "normal" ("Welcome,"
screen 1). Yet, since the mid-1990s, Jamaica—with a population of approximately 2.8 million—has experienced an unprecedented wave of violence,
mostly in the form of gang-related slayings. In 1997, an estimated 1,038
Jamaicans were murdered, the highest number of murders ever recorded in
a single year in Jamaica (Webster, screen 1). By September of 2000, more
than 600 people had already died in gang-related violence ("Jamaican's Eye"
A6). Jamaica's homicide rate, some experts estimate, was twenty times
higher than that of London ("Welcome," screen 1) or equivalent to 100,000
murders a year in the United States (Vulliamy, screen 1).

Except for Jamaica's tiny wealthy class and the foreign tourists who
inhabit the posh all-inclusive resorts on Jamaica's celebrated North Coast,
no one has been immune to the violence. The victims have ranged from
young schoolchildren to the elderly, from the poorest segments of the population to the middle class. In one case, members of a Jamaican gang, commonly called "Yardies" or "Dons," gang-raped a seventeen-year-old girl and
murdered her by slashing her throat and burned her face "beyond recogni-
tion." More recently, a Jamaican gang used a "variation on the guillotine,"
forcing its victim to "kneel with his head on the rim of a car truck as the lid
was slammed shut" (Vulliamy, screens 1–2).

Literally fearing for their lives, the Jamaican middle class have left
Jamaica in record numbers for the United States, Canada, and Great Britain.
The British High Commission reported that immigration applications rose
an average of 21 percent annually from 1997 to 2000 (Rosenberg, "Hard
Times" B4). Beyond threats of violence, many middle-class Jamaicans have
fared poorly during Jamaica's recent economic crisis. Some have lost their
private-sector jobs, while others—small business owners—have watched
their fortunes vanish or lost their businesses altogether. Barry Chevannes

summed up the cause for the exodus of Jamaica's middle class: "People are fed up with high levels of violence and the deep recession that the economy is in, without any prospect of turning around" (qtd. in Rosenberg, "Hard Times" B4).

Observers have speculated on the causes for this recent upswing of violence. Writing in the *New Republic,* reporter Ed Vulliamy traced the violence back to the 1970s, when the two warring political parties "armed citizens to create what were called political 'garrisons' in the ghetto—in effect, military wings of each party's election machinery" (screens 1–2). After the defeat of Michael Manley's democratic socialist government in 1980, the gangs, according to the *Economist,* deserted the political parties and started to "make money from drugs and extortion" ("Welcome," screen 1).

Other observers have suggested that a 1996 banking crisis has contributed to the escalation of violence in Jamaica. In a failed attempt to bail out banks as well as insurance and investment companies, the Jamaican government borrowed heavily, an estimated one billion dollars, from international sources. The bailout, experts suggest, had a ripple effect throughout Jamaica: interest rates skyrocketed to nearly 40 percent, small businesses closed or declared bankruptcy, and unemployment jumped to an estimated 25 percent. This economic crisis left Jamaica's youth population to fend for themselves, and many turned to crime as a means of survival (Rosenberg, "Hard Times" B4).

The response to the rise in violence has been swift, but quite unsuccessful. Dubbed "Operation Intrepid," the Jamaican government and its security forces seized eighty-five firearms, two thousand rounds of ammunition, and arrested sixty-five criminals in 1999 on charges ranging from rape to murder (Webster, screen 1). In July 1999, the violence was so intense that Jamaica augmented its police force with its military after "a week in which more than 10 people were murdered and hundreds of residents fled their homes fearing for their lives" ("Jamaican Troops," screen 1). During the summer of 2001, Prime Minister P. J. Patterson activated

over three thousand troops to quell seemingly politically motivated violence ("Jamaica Officials" A4). The violence, resulting in at least seven-
ty-one deaths and hundreds being injured, was concentrated primarily in
West Kingston communities controlled by gangs ("Seven Die" A10; "At
Least," screen 1).

In addition to the government's anti-crime initiatives, new political par-
ties have formed, promising to halt the spread of violence. In 1995, Bruce
Golding, former chairperson of the JLP, left his party to form the National
Democratic Movement (NDM). If elected, the NDM promised the
Jamaican people ten "covenants," including the removal of "the scourge of
crime and violence and the wanton waste of the lives of our people"
(*National Democratic Movement*, screen 1).

Amidst the violence that has plagued Jamaica in recent years, reggae music
is making a resurgence in Jamaica. By the mid-1980s, the Jamaica youth largely abandoned reggae music for new genres of Jamaican music, alternatively
called "dancehall," "ragga," and "digital." These new genres of music were
mostly noted, and largely criticized, for their preoccupation with dope, guns,
violence, and casual sex. The shift from dancehall music to the spiritual,
Rastafarian-influenced "roots" reggae music began in the mid-1990s when
dancehall artists, such as Grammy-award winner Shabba Ranks, started to
grow dreadlocks and sing familiar Rastafarian themes of spirituality and social
justice. Carlene J. Edie, associate professor of political science at the University of Massachusetts, Amherst, observed that the wave of political violence
has encouraged Jamaicans to seek "religious options now, because the political parties seem to have failed everybody. . . . I'm not surprised to hear that
this is showing up in the music" (qtd. in Wexler, screen 2).

It is not surprising that reggae music has reemerged during this time of
violence and corruption in Jamaica, for reggae was "created by Jamaicans
to satisfy their spiritual and emotional needs" (Chang and Chen 2). As
compelling evidence for this claim, reggae music (and Jamaican music in
general) remains one of the only outlets for the Jamaican masses, especially the poor, to express their collective voice in society. In addition,

reggae music has helped many Jamaicans understand and appreciate their African ancestry. Reggae music also gave voice to the Rastafarian ethos and helped popularize the movement in Jamaica and throughout the world. Yet, at the same time, the Jamaican establishment and its surrogates co-opted the images of reggae music and the symbols of the Rastafarian movement, most notably for the promotion of Jamaica's growing tourist industry.

CONCLUSION

Nobody is scared of Rasta anymore; it's accepted; it's something that people look at with more seriousness now. Those things have been won.

—Ibo Cooper

The Rastafarian movement is no longer considered a threat to Jamaica's domestic tranquility or national security. Instead, it has been co-opted into a symbol of Jamaica's cultural heritage and transformed into a tourist attraction. How this came about has implications for understanding social movements and music as a medium of protest. Although unique in some ways, the history of the Rastafarian movement has implications for all social movements that rely on music as a means of expression.

RASTAFARI AND SOCIAL MOVEMENT THEORY

While the Rastafarians exhibited some of the traditional characteristics of a social movement, the unique characteristics of this movement raise interesting questions about social movement theory. Unlike most social movements, the Rastafarians resisted the temptation to centralize and unify around a dominant leader. Indeed, the Rastafarian movement never really had a central leader or even a written doctrine. The decentralized nature of the movement played a key role in the Rastafarians' ability to flourish when its leaders were deported or jailed, or when its protest messages were banned from the public airwaves. In the 1960s, for example, the imprisonment of Rastafarian "leader" Claudius Henry and the deportation of black nationalist and University of the West Indies (UWI) professor Walter Rodney had little effect on the movement. Without a single, identifiable leader to target, the Jamaican government and its supporters lacked effective means to stem the growth of the movement, and the Rastafarians continued to gain popularity and sympathy from Jamaica's lower classes throughout the 1960s.

At the same time, however, the lack of a clear organizational structure may have made the movement more vulnerable to co-optation. As the popularity of reggae music grew internationally in the 1970s, the movement became even more fragmented, more diverse, and even less unified around religious or political tenets. Without a central leader to unify the various groups, the Rastafarians became vulnerable to pseudo-Rastafarians claiming to speak for the movement. More traditional Rastafarians resisted the government's token concessions and the commercial exploitation of the movement and its music, but a sufficient number of Rastafarians benefited from these changes to blunt the movement's political edge. Yet, many reggae musicians who have been blamed for the commercialization of the movement were themselves victims of Manley's failed attempt to restructure Jamaica's economy in the 1970s. Indeed, reggae musicians were often forced to play for "profit" as a means of economic survival. Thus, the severe decline of the Jamaican economy after 1976 may have had some effect on the increasing commercialization of the Rastafarian movement.

The Rastafarians' reliance on music as its chief form of political dissent also has implications for social movement theory. This study illustrates how music might serve as an effective vehicle to recruit new followers or sympathizers to a cause (commonly referred to as "identity marketing"). According to communication scholars James R. Irvine and Walter G. Kirkpatrick listeners do not readily identify music as argumentative or persuasive and thus may be "ready recipients" of the rhetorical appeal of a song "without being aware of its complete implications." Attracted to music as "entertainment," listeners may be less prepared to reject its verbal message (273). Reggae's unique combination of protest lyrics and a tranquil sound—what cultural critic Dick Hebdige has called a "classic Caribbean package of bitter social commentary wrapped up in a light, refreshing rhythm"—represented a uniquely enticing and subtle form of social protest (*Cut* 81). With the rage of its lyrics softened by its soothing, even hypnotic sound, reggae invited some listeners to lose themselves in the *feel* of the Rastafarian/reggae culture.

Yet music, as a mode of protest, may be especially vulnerable to co-optation. Michael Manley and the People's National Party (PNP) apparently had little trouble enticing reggae bands to play at political rallies during the 1972 national election. Similarly, few reggae musicians could resist the opportunity to become international "stars," even if that meant the commercialization of their music. Some Rastafarian traditionalists were horrified by the role of reggae music in Jamaica's political elections, and traditionalists also criticized reggae musicians for commercializing the movement. Nevertheless, reggae musicians willingly participated in the transformation of reggae music into a cultural commodity. The critics were probably right: more and more started playing for "profit" rather than for spiritual or political purposes.

The question still remains: Can music really communicate serious ideological content? According to communication scholar Ralph E. Knupp, the answer is no, since music thrives on "ambiguities, sweeping assertions, and panoramic criticisms rather than on specific issues, policies, and arguments" (384–5). Bob Marley's "Exodus," for example, invoked such familiar

Rastafarian terms as "Jah People," "exodus," "Father's land," and "Babylon," yet it hardly critiqued the government or made the case for repatriation. In some measure, Knupp's point seems confirmed by this study: reggae attracted large numbers of devotees to the imagery and symbolism of Rastafari, but few of these "pseudo-Rastafarians" grasped the complexities of the movement's religious practices and/or political goals.

The internationalization of the Rastafarian movement also has implications for social movement theory. Social movement theorists have not examined the unique challenges faced by "international" social movements. Despite the Rastafarians' growing popularity, the internationalization of the movement created pseudo-Rastafarian groups—groups comprised of followers who did not embrace the movement's religious practices or political goals. The proliferation of pseudo-Rastafarian groups increasingly fragmented an already decentralized movement. More important, Rastafarian symbols— once unique to Jamaica—now could be reinterpreted by the international Rastafarian community. For example, the Ethiopian Zion Coptic Church's exploitation of marijuana trivialized the claim that marijuana was used for religious and spiritual purposes. In short, international social movements face unique challenges that other social movements may not experience.

The strategies to "control" the Rastafarian movement have implications for the study of the rhetoric of control. Scholars contend that the strategies of control typically escalate from the mild to the more repressive (Bowers, Ochs, and Jensen 49). The decentralized nature of the Rastafarian movement, however, forced the Jamaican government and its surrogates to employ a variety of different strategies simultaneously to "control" the movement. Nevertheless, the Jamaican government failed to stem the Rastafarian's political activism and growing popularity in Jamaica. This study questions the assumption that establishments use control strategies in sequential order. This study also suggests that the unique characteristics of a social movement may determine how establishments employ these strategies of control.

Similarly, social movement theorists have suggested that after the failure of "evasion," "counter-persuasion," "coercion," and "adjustment" strategies, establishment's simply "capitulate" to the demands of a social movement (Bowers, Ochs, and Jensen 63). Yet, as this study has demonstrated, the Jamaican establishment did not capitulate to the Rastafarian movement. Instead, the Jamaican establishment "co-opted" the cultural symbols of Rastafari and reggae music as authentic symbols of Jamaican society. Perhaps the Jamaican establishment employed an intermediate control method, "co-optation," to give the illusion of victory. This study suggests that "co-optation" *may* be a separate strategy in itself—a necessary strategy when all other attempts have failed to control a social movement. Future researchers should explore whether co-optation is an adjustment "tactic" or a new "strategy" of social control.

How this came about has additional implications for understanding social movements and the rhetoric of social control. First, our understanding of social control as a rhetorical phenomenon reflects an American/British cultural bias (Lucas 265). Since most social movement case studies are centered in North America and Europe, social movement theorists have not typically examined how colonialism (or neo-colonialism) serves as the establishment's chief ideology of control. According to political scientist John Wilson, the existing model of control depicts control agents (i.e., security forces) enforcing policies established by a target group (i.e., government). The target group is the "group a social movement is in conflict with" (471).[1]

The traditional model may be represented by this diagram (figure E.1):

TARGET GROUP (Jamaican Government)	CONTROL AGENTS (Security Forces)
SOCIAL MOVEMENT (Rastafarian Movement)	

Yet, the traditional model fails to accurately depict the historical experience of (neo)colonialism in Jamaica. Thus, it is important to distinguish between an "external" target group, an outside entity with the legitimate power to influence another country's political, social, and cultural policies, and an "internal" target group, a local governing body. The new model (called the external control model) may be represented by this diagram (figure E.2):

```
┌─────────────────────────────────────────────────────────────────────┐
│                         EXTERNAL TARGET GROUP                         │
│                   (Great Britain/international community)             │
│                                                                       │
│                                                                       │
│  INTERNAL TARGET GROUP                               CONTROL AGENTS   │
│  (Jamaican Government)                               (Security Forces)│
│                                                                       │
│                          SOCIAL MOVEMENT                              │
│                       (Rastafarian Movement)                          │
└─────────────────────────────────────────────────────────────────────┘
```

In the 1960s, the Jamaican government (internal target group) and its surrogates perpetuated a neo-colonial stratification system, encouraging its citizens to emulate British culture (external target group). Jamaica's citizens, especially the ruling classes, denigrated any "Jamaican" or "African" artifact as "backward," "primitive," or "unsophisticated." The Rastafarian movement—with its allegiance to Africa and its demands for repatriation—challenged this neo-colonial stratification system. Similarly, Jamaica's popular music contested the image of an island paradise by highlighting the racial injustice and economic poverty in Jamaica.

By the early 1970s, Jamaica's new political leadership (internal target group) and the popularity of reggae and Rastafari signaled, at first glance, the end of neo-colonialism in Jamaica. Recognizing Jamaica's African heritage and implementing new economic policies, Manley seemed to censure Jamaica's neo-colonial stratification system. Furthermore, the growing international acceptance of reggae played a significant role in the popularity of the Rastafarian movement. With the international stamp of approval (external target group), Jamaicans began to view reggae music and the Rastafarian movement as important and positive symbols of Jamaica's cultural heritage. Despite Manley's new democratic socialist government and the "acceptance" of reggae and the Rastafarian movement, a neo-colonial social structure continued to exist in Jamaica during the 1970s.

Conclusion

It is important to recognize the external target group's role in perpetuating a neo-colonial social structure in Jamaica. Under colonial rule, Great Britain's influence was profound, reaching virtually every area of Jamaican society. Not only did Great Britain have the right to exercise authority over Jamaica's internal affairs, but this colonial power established the normative cultural practices in Jamaica. Great Britain created what Barry Chevannes called the "ideology of racism" in Jamaica ("Healing" 62). In this social system, Great Britain established the norms for acceptable skin color, body norms, and moral character. Yet, even after Jamaica's independence from Great Britain and the rise of Manley's socialist government, the Jamaican public, particularly the middle class, deferred to the international community (external target group) to validate the importance of reggae and the Rastafarian movement to Jamaica's cultural heritage. In sum, an external target group—albeit a more benign one—has continued to influence and legitimize Jamaica's political, social, and cultural practices.

This study also rejects attempts to reduce the definition of social control to a series of "turf wars" between control agents and protestors (Wilson 470–1). While control agents are an important part of the process of maintaining power and social order, establishment's often lend both nonrhetorical and rhetorical strategies to curb social protest. As Herbert W. Simons has suggested, social control is rhetorical and physical, ideological and material (*Persuasion* 253). As noted above, Great Britain rhetorically constructed the "ideology of racism" to control Jamaica's political, social, and cultural policies. While Jamaica's security forces defended this ideology by physically punishing the Rastafarians and the poor, the political establishment, the media, and the middle class sustained and perpetuated this ideology through public communication and shared symbols. Thus, social control can be defined as any effort to maintain or sustain an external or internal target group's ideology, legitimacy, and/or power.

To maintain its power and legitimacy, the Jamaican establishment and its surrogates used co-optation as a strategy to control the Rastafarians. Although co-optation has been neglected, for the most part, as an important area of study for social movement scholars, this study offers new insights into the co-optation strategy. First, scholars have not examined how target groups co-opt social movement leaders.[2] Since the Rastafarian movement lacked a central leader, the Jamaican establishment co-opted the religious, political, and cultural symbols of the movement. In several recent interviews, Rastafarian and reggae scholars, including Barry Chevannes, acknowledged that Rastafarian symbols have, in part, been "co-opted" by Jamaica's dominant classes. Indeed, Manley and his supporters embraced the external trappings of Rastafari—the locks and reggae itself—but threatened to reduce Rastafari to little more than a cultural fad. This study suggests that establishments can co-opt both leaders and symbols of a social movement. While contributing to social movement theory, this study also provides important contributions to the study of protest music.

REGGAE AND PROTEST MUSIC THEORY

While rhetorical scholars have examined thoroughly the rhetorical functions of protest music, few, if any, have studied protest music as an evolving rhetorical phenomenon. As we have seen, Jamaica's protest music evolved from ska, a passive, apolitical music, to reggae, a more aggressive, even violent protest music. While ska musicians sang about the social conditions in the Jamaican ghettoes, the music expressed more "personal" rather than "political" themes. In contrast, reggae music addressed specific social problems (e.g., political violence) while calling for violent strategies to overcome oppression in Jamaica. Not surprisingly, American black music—from gospel to R&B and blues to rap—reflected a similar rhetorical evolution. Based on this case study, protest music seems to evolve from the "personal" to the "political," from passive to aggressive messages of protest. This study encourages scholars to examine other musical genres as the basis for creating a model for the rhetorical stages of protest music.

Furthermore, scholars have failed to examine the establishment's role in the rhetorical evolution of protest music. From 1959 to 1980, the Jamaican government played a pivotal role in banning controversial protest music from the public airwaves. At the same time, the government promoted the island's indigenous music overseas, hired reggae bands to play at political rallies, and exploited reggae imagery for economic and promotional goals. Similarly, the broadcast media promoted a middle-class "pop" version of Jamaican music, while banning songs deemed too "radical" and "political" for Jamaica's public airwaves. During the 1960s, international record companies such as Trojan Records marketed a domesticated or "pop" version of Jamaican popular music to international audiences. While efforts to promote "pop" reggae failed to attract new and larger audiences, Island Records President Chris Blackwell perfected his strategy in the 1970s, augmenting one of Jamaica's more controversial reggae bands, the Wailers, with a new sound and a new image. In all cases, the establishment—from the government to the broadcast media to international record companies—banned, promoted, modified, and even co-opted Jamaica's protest music. The Jamaican political establishment thus played a significant role in the evolution of reggae music.

Rhetorical scholars have also failed to examine how different protest songs communicate mixed, often contradictory, messages to audiences. Some reggae songs, for example, advocated immediate repatriation to Africa while other songs suggested political reform in Jamaica. Likewise, some reggae songs advocated the themes of "peace" and "unity," while other songs called for more violent, more aggressive strategies to overcome oppression in Jamaica. This study not only confirms Knupp's observation that protest music may not be an effective medium to communicate serious ideological content, but questions the assumption that protest music presents congruous messages to audiences.

In the end, the Rastafarian movement achieved few of its concrete goals, such as legalizing marijuana, reforming Jamaica's economic or political system, or repatriation to Africa. However, this movement has left a permanent mark on Jamaica's cultural landscape. As a social movement, Rastafari thus succeeded in symbolic terms; what once had been a mysterious religious "cult" in a small Caribbean island redefined that nation's cultural identity and became an international phenomenon. The movement's use of Jamaica's popular music suggests that, while music may be an effective medium for popularizing a social movement, it has limitations as a mode of ideological discourse and may make movements more vulnerable to co-optation.

NOTES

Introduction

1. See, for example, Leonard E. Barrett, *The Rastafarians: Sounds of Cultural Dissonance*, Rev. ed. (Boston: Beacon, 1988); Horace Campbell, *Rasta and Resistance: From Marcus Garvey to Walter Rodney* (Trenton: Africa World, 1987); Barry Chevannes, *Rastafari: Roots and Ideology* (New York: Syracuse UP, 1994); Obika Gray, *Radicalism and Social Change in Jamaica, 1960–1972* (Knoxville: U of Tennessee P, 1991); Rex M. Nettleford, *Identity, Race and Protest in Jamaica* (New York: William Morrow, 1972); Joseph Owens, *Dread: The Rastafarians of Jamaica* (Kingston, JA: Sangster, 1976); Anita M. Waters, *Race, Class, and Political Symbols: Rastafari and Reggae in Jamaican Politics* (New Brunswick: Transaction, 1985).

2. See, for example, Dick Hebdige, *Cut 'N' Mix: Culture, Identity and Caribbean Music* (New York: Methuen, 1987); Simon Jones, *Black Culture, White Youth: The Reggae Tradition from JA to UK* (Houndmills, Eng.: Macmillan, 1988).

3. See, for example, Obika Gray, *Radicalism and Social Change in Jamaica, 1960–1972* (Knoxville: U of Tennessee P, 1991); Terry Lacey, *Violence and Politics in Jamaica, 1960–70: Internal Security in a Developing Country* (Totowa: Frank Cass, 1977).

Chapter One

1. Mento emerged in the 1930s and is generally characterized by its experimentation with European (trumpet) and African (drums) instruments. While mento was heard throughout Jamaica, it is largely a rural-based music. See, for example, Garth White,

Notes

Traditional Musical Practice in Jamaica and Its Influence on the Birth of Modern Jamaican Popular Music (Kingston, JA: African-Caribbean Institute of Jamaica, 1982).

2. Rastafarians also use "reasoning," an informal dialectic, to debate issues and seek wisdom.

3. From 1940 to 1952, the PNP espoused socialism until the more conservative members of the PNP convinced Norman Manley that the party's extreme left wing, a group of self-proclaimed Marxists, were a threat to his authority. In 1952, Manley expelled the four Marxists, popularly known as the four H's—Ken and Frank Hill, Richard Hart, and Arthur Henry—from the party. For the next twenty years, the PNP would remain dedicated to a liberal, democratic policy until Norman Manley's son, Michael Manley, reintroduced the political philosophy of democratic socialism in 1974. See, for example, Carl Stone, "Power, Policy and Politics in Independent Jamaica," *Jamaica in Independence: Essays on the Early Years,* ed. Rex Nettleford (Kingston, JA: Heinemann Caribbean, 1989), 21.

4. In 1961, Norman Manley decided to send delegates (from the Rastafarian movement and a governmental council) to search for land in Africa. The committee traveled to five African states to experiment with the idea of emigration and eventual citizenship. Unfortunately, for the Rastafarian movement, the "first official mission to Africa" (1961) and a nongovernment-sponsored "second mission to Africa" (1963–1965) did not result in achieving the movement's goal of repatriation. See *Majority Report of Mission to Africa* (Kingston, JA: Government Printer, 1961) and Douglas R. A. Mack, *From Babylon to Rastafari: Origin and History of the Rastafarian Movement* (Chicago: Research Associates School Times Publications and Frontline Distribution International, 1999).

5. For the Jamaican DJ, the term "toasting" often refers to sexual bragging.

6. According to Caribbean music expert Kenneth M. Bilby, the "influence of mento, in particular, has been underrated. Not only would some argue that the characteristic ska afterbeat actually stems in part from the strumming patterns of the banjo or guitar in mento, but ska versions of traditional mento tunes were common during the early 1960s" ("Jamaica" 29). Bilby also suggests that the mento influence actually "increased during the reggae era" and that "[f]ew listeners outside of Jamaica know that there was a whole substyle or genre of mento-reggae (sometimes called 'country music') that enjoyed tremendous popularity in the island during the 1970s" (30).

7. The beat, according to the *New Grove Dictionary of Jazz,* is "[t]he basic pulse underlying measured music and thus the unit by which musical time is reckoned; the beat, though not always sounded, is always perceived as underpinning the temporal progress of the music, and it is only the presence of the beat that allows rhythm to be established" (Kernfeld 85).

8. The following is a nontechnical description of quarter notes, eighth notes, and sixteenth notes: Using a heartbeat as an example of a steady rhythm, four consecutive beats represent a typical bar or measure of music. Count and repeat the numerical sequence: (*1 2 3 4 1 2 3 4 1 2*, etc.). Each beat is called a quarter note. The upbeats

146

or offbeats exist "half-way" between each beat, yielding eight notes to a bar, thus the term "eighth note." This beat is identified by an "&," and can be represented by the following illustration (1 & 2 & 3 & 4 & 1 & 2, etc.). Dividing each of these eight notes in half produces sixteenth notes. This is illustrated in the following way (1 e & a 2 e & a 3 e & a 4 e & a 1 e & a, etc.). Of course, musicians can further subdivide the beat and are free to combine these rhythms with rests or silence to create infinite forms of expression.

Chapter Two

1. Because of the limitations of the recording technology, the bass drum was often inaudible in many rocksteady recordings.
2. Music writer Katherine Charlton defined call and response as the "practice of singing in which a solo vocalist, the caller, is answered by a group of singers. The practice is also used with instruments, but its origins are vocal" (262).

Chapter Three

1. In 1962, the JLP established the "Five Year Plan" to increase economic ties to the West and foreign investment in Jamaica.
2. By the 1970s, the Jamaican dollar was "slightly at better than parity to the US dollar" (Manley, *Jamaica* 160). However, in recent years, the Jamaican dollar has undergone a destabilization process and lost much of its initial worth. For example, in July 1994, the exchange rate was J$32 to US$1. Seven years later, the exchange rate was J$45 to US$1.
3. According to the book entitled *Modern Recording Techniques*, this technique allows a musician to "play or sing along with himself [or herself] to make his [or her] performance sound fuller or so that an effect can be created. The musician listens to his [or her] original performance and tries to match its phrasing as he [or she] overdubs. The two tracks are then played back together. This technique is called *doubling*" (343-4).

Chapter Five

1. A number of sources and, at least, one former CIA agent have confirmed Manley's contention that the CIA was intimately involved in the destabilization of the PNP government during the 1970s. According to former CIA officer Philip Agee, the CIA "was using the Jamaica Labour Party as its instrument in the entire campaign against the Michael Manley government. I'd say most of the violence was coming from the Jamaica Labour Party side, and behind them was the CIA in terms of getting the weapons in and getting the money in" (*Bob Marley: Rebel Music*).
2. According to Michael Manley, the IMF deal forced Jamaica to devalue its dollar from "a position slightly at better than parity to the US dollar to an exchange rate of J$1.76 for US$1.00" (*Jamaica* 160).

3. According to Barry Chevannes, not all of Jamaica's middle class were defecting to the Rastafarian faith: "Not only the working class youths, but the middle classes as well were now defining themselves closer to the Rasta than to the white reference point. . . . This does not mean that the middle-class is becoming Rasta. Far from it. But it does signify a tendency to identify more with the African reference point than with the European" ("Healing" 78–9).

Chapter Six

1. See, for example, Aggrey Brown, *Color, Class, and Politics in Jamaica* (New Brunswick: Transaction, 1979); Joseph Owens, *Dread: The Rastafarians of Jamaica* (Kingston, JA: Sangster, 1976); Rex M. Nettleford, *Identity, Race and Protest in Jamaica* (New York: William Morrow, 1972); Carole D. Yawney, "Remnants of All Nations: Rastafarian Attitudes to Race and Nationality," *Ethnicity in the Americas*, ed. Francis Henry (Hague: Mouton, 1976), 231–66.
2. Under the JLP government, possession of marijuana for first-time offenders carried a minimum sentence of eighteen months. Under Manley's revised marijuana laws, a standard minimum sentence for possession was abolished and the maximum sentence for a first conviction was reduced to three years (Fraser 373–4).
3. Reggae musicians were often forced to pay disc jockeys a monetary fee, often called payola, to have a song played on the radio. If a musician did not have enough money or refused to pay the required fee, physical intimidation became a popular persuasive tactic. According to Dermot Hussey, a former employee of RJR and JBC, disc jockeys frequently became targets of physical intimidation. Struggling musicians, according to Hussey, often "resort[ed] to roughing people [DJs]."

Epilogue

1. Despite the success of Sumfest, "the festival scene is not what it used to be; where crowds once reached 30,000 nightly, even Sumfest is lucky to draw 20,000 today. As artist fees have risen—peaking at J$1 million for DJ Beenie Man in 1996—so ticket prices have become prohibitive for many Jamaicans, who increasingly prefer to attend sound-system jams rather than live shows" (Thomas, Vaitilingam, and Vaitilingham, screen 2).
2. See, for example, James Hamlyn, *Fodor's Exploring Caribbean*, 2nd ed. (New York: Fodor's Travel, 1996); Karl Luntta, *Jamaica Handbook*, 2nd ed. (Chico: Moon, 1993); Paris Permenter and John Bigley, *Caribbean for Lovers* (Rocklin: Prima, 1997); Darwin Porter and Danforth Prince, *Frommer's Jamaica and Barbados*, 3rd ed. (New York: Simon and Schuster, 1996).
3. As expected, Rastafari and reggae images have been exported to other Caribbean countries—from Grand Bahama Island to Grand Cayman Island. In many of these tourist areas, visitors can buy merchandise (e.g., tee-shirts, hats, coffee cups, shot glasses) imprinted with reggae/Rastafari imagery.

4. Pruitt and LaFont distinguish "romantic tourism" from "sex tourism." While sex tourism "serves to perpetuate gender roles and reinforce power relations of male dominance and female subordination," romance tourism involves women "traveling in pursuit of relationships." The authors assert, however, that romance tourism is not merely the act of "role reversal." Instead of perceiving themselves as prostitutes, the "actors place an emphasis on courtship rather than the exchange of sex for money" (423).

Conclusion

1. See, for example, William A. Gamson, *Power and Discontent* (Homewood: Dorsey, 1968); Andrew A. King, "The Rhetoric of Power Maintenance: Elites at the Precipice," *Quarterly Journal of Speech* 62 (1976): 127–34; Herbert W. Simons, *Persuasion: Understanding, Practice, and Analysis* (Reading: Addison-Wesley, 1976); Charles J. Stewart, Craig Allen Smith, and Robert E. Denton Jr., *Persuasion and Social Movements*, 3rd ed. (Prospect Heights: Waveland, 1994).
2. As Wilson has argued, however, this might not always be the case: "[E]ven where structural links between a social movement's target group (e.g., a State Board of Education) and agents of social control (e.g., State Police) can be demonstrated, it does not follow that they act as one. There are large areas within any government bureaucracy for agents of social control to play autonomous roles" (471).

WORKS CITED

Books and Pamphlets

Adams, Emilie L. *Understanding Jamaican Patois: An Introduction to Afro-Jamaican Grammar*. Kingston, JA: Kingston Publishers, 1991.

Adventure Tours USA: Sun Escapes. Dallas: Adventure Tours, n.d.

Ahkell, Jah. *Rasta: Emperor Haile Selassie and the Rastafarians*. Port of Spain: Black Starliner, 1981.

Air Jamaica. Kingston, JA: Air Jamaica, 1995/1996.

Alleyne, Mervyn C. *Roots of Jamaican Culture*. London: Pluto, 1988.

Barrett, Leonard E. *The Rastafarians: Sounds of Cultural Dissonance*. Rev. ed. Boston: Beacon, 1988.

Beckford, George, and Michael Witter. *Small Garden . . . Bitter Weed: The Political Economy of Struggle and Change in Jamaica*. Morant Bay, JA: Maroon, 1982.

Berry, Mary Frances, and John W. Blassingame. *Long Memory: The Black Experience in America*. New York: Oxford UP, 1982.

Bilby, Kenneth. "Jamaica." *Reggae, Rasta, Revolution: Jamaican Music from Ska to Dub*. Edited by Chris Potash. New York: Schirmer, 1997. 29–36.

———. "The Caribbean as a Musical Region." *Caribbean Contours*. Edited by Sidney Mintz and Sally Price. Baltimore: Johns Hopkins UP, 1985. 1–38.

Boot, Adrian, and Michael Thomas. *Jamaica: Babylon on a Thin Wire*. London: Thames and Hudson, 1976.

Bowers, John W., Donovan J. Ochs, and Richard J. Jensen. *The Rhetoric of Agitation and Control*. 2nd ed. Prospect Heights: Waveland, 1993.

Works Cited

Boyd, Derick A. C. *Economic Management, Income Distribution, and Poverty in Jamaica.* New York: Praeger, 1988.

Brodber, Erna. "Socio-cultural Change in Jamaica." *Jamaica in Independence: Essays on the Early Years.* Edited by Rex Nettleford. Kingston, JA: Heinemann Caribbean, 1989. 55–74.

Brodber, Erna, and J. Edward Greene. *Reggae and Cultural Identity in Jamaica.* U of the West Indies, JA: Institute of Social and Economic Research, 1981.

Brown, Aggrey. *Color, Class, and Politics in Jamaica.* New Brunswick, N.J.: Transaction, 1979.

———. "Mass Communication and the Practice of Radical Politics in Jamaica." *Perspectives on Jamaica in the Seventies.* Edited by Carl Stone and Aggrey Brown. Kingston, JA: Jamaican Publishing House, 1981. 301–7.

———. "Mass Media in Jamaica." *Mass Media and the Caribbean.* Edited by Stuart H. Surlin and Walter C. Soderlund. New York: Gordon and Breach, 1990. 11–28.

C, Gordon. *The Reggae Files.* London: Hansib, 1988.

Campbell, Horace. *Bob Marley Lives: Reggae, Rasta and Resistance.* Dar es Salaam, Traz.: Tackey, 1981.

———. *Rasta and Resistance: From Marcus Garvey to Walter Rodney.* Trenton: Africa World, 1987.

Carpenter, Bill. "Gospel." *All Music Guide: The Best CDs, Albums, and Tapes.* Edited by Michael Erlewine and Scott Bultman. San Francisco: Miller Freeman, 1992. 405.

Chang, Kevin O'Brien, and Wayne Chen. *Reggae Routes: The Story of Jamaican Music.* Philadelphia: Temple UP, 1998.

Charles, Pearnel. *Detained.* Kingston, JA: Kingston Publishers, 1978.

Charlton, Katherine. *Rock Music Styles: A History.* Dubuque, Iowa: Wm. C. Brown, 1990.

Chevannes, Barry. *Rastafari: Roots and Ideology.* New York: Syracuse UP, 1994.

———. "The Rastafari and the Urban Youth." *Perspectives on Jamaica in the Seventies.* Edited by Carl Stone and Aggrey Brown. Kingston, JA: Jamaica Publishing House, 1981. 392–422.

Clarke, Sebastian. *Jah Music: The Evolution of the Popular Jamaican Song.* London: Heinemann, 1980.

Davis, Stephen. *Bob Marley.* London: Panther, 1983.

———. "Bob Marley—A Final Interview." *Reggae International.* Edited by Stephen Davis and Peter Simon. New York: Rogner and Bernhard, 1982. 88–91.

———. "Talking Drums, Sound Systems and Reggae." *Reggae International.* Edited by Stephen Davis and Peter Simon. New York: Rogner and Bernhard, 1982. 33–4.

Davis, Stephen, and Peter Simon, eds. *Reggae Bloodlines: In Search of the Music and Culture of Jamaica.* New York: Anchor/Doubleday, 1977. New York: Da Capo, 1992.

Davis, Stephen, and Peter Simon. "A Rasta Glossary." *Reggae International.* Edited by Stephen Davis and Peter Simon. New York: Rogner and Bernhard, 1982. 69.

Dempsey, Mary, and Delinda Karle. *Access Caribbean.* 3rd ed. New York: Harper Collins, 1996.

Diedrichs, Gary. *Fodor's 92: Jamaica.* New York: Fodor's Travel, 1992.

Works Cited

Ehrlich, Luke. "The Reggae Arrangement." *Reggae International*. Edited by Stephen Davis and Peter Simon. New York: Rogner and Bernhard, 1982. 52–5.

Fanon, Frantz. *The Wretched of the Earth*. New York: Grove, 1968.

Ferguson, Bryan J. "Selected Historical Events in the Evolution of Rastafari." *Arise Ye Mighty People!: Gender, Class and Race in Popular Struggles*. Edited by Terisa E. Turner with Bryan J. Ferguson. Trenton: Africa World, 1994. 57–64.

Fergusson, Isaac. "'So Much Things to Say': The Journey of Bob Marley." *Reggae, Rasta, Revolution: Jamaican Music from Ska to Dub*. Edited by Chris Potash. New York: Schirmer, 1997. 51–60.

Forsythe, Dennis. *Rastafari: For the Healing of the Nation*. Kingston, JA: Ziaka, 1983.

Friedland, Ed. *Reggae Bass*. Milwaukee, Wisc.: Hal Leonard, 1998.

Gamson, William A. *Power and Discontent*. Homewood: Dorsey, 1968.

Gillett, Charlie. *The Sound of the City: The Rise of Rock and Roll*. New York: Outerbridge & Dienstfrey, 1970.

Grass, Randall. "Rock Steady into Reggae, 1968–1972." *Reggae International*. Edited by Stephen Davis and Peter Simon. New York: Rogner and Bernhard, 1982. 45–7.

Gray, Obika. *Radicalism and Social Change in Jamaica, 1960–1972*. Knoxville: U of Tennessee P, 1991.

Hamlyn, James. *Fodor's Exploring Caribbean*. 2nd ed. New York: Fodor's Travel, 1996.

Hebdige, Dick. *Cut 'N' Mix: Culture, Identity and Caribbean Music*. New York: Methuen, 1987.

———. *Subculture: The Meaning of Style*. London: Routledge, 1988.

Hitchins, Ray. *The Reggae Riddim: Essential Information for All Reggae Musicians*. Milwaukee, Wisc.: Hal Leonard, 1996.

Jacobs, Virginia Lee. *Roots of Rastafari*. San Diego: Avant, 1985.

Jahn, Brian, and Tom Weber. *Reggae Island: Jamaican Music in the Digital Age*. Kingston, JA: Kingston Publishers, 1992.

Jamaica. Kingston, JA: Jamaica Tourist Board, 1997.

Jamaica-Jamaica. Runaway Bay, JA: Jamaica-Jamaica, n.d.

Jones, Simon. *Black Culture, White Youth: The Reggae Tradition from Jamaica to the United Kingdom*. Houndmills, Eng.: Macmillan Education, 1988.

Kernfeld, Barry. "Beat." *The New Grove Dictionary of Jazz*. Edited by Barry Kernfeld. New York: St. Martin's, 1995. 85–8.

King, A. *A Look at the Black Struggle in Jamaica*. Kingston, JA: Black House, 1969.

Kuper, Adam: *Changing Jamaica*. London: Routledge & Kegan Paul, 1976.

Lacey, Terry. *Violence and Politics in Jamaica, 1960–70: Internal Security in a Developing Country*. Totowa: Frank Cass, 1977.

Lee, Barbara Makeda. *Rastafari: The New Creation*. Kingston, JA: Jamaica Media, 1981.

Luntta, Karl. *Jamaica Handbook*. 2nd ed. Chico: Moon, 1993.

Mack, Douglas R. A. *From Babylon to Rastafari: Origin and History of the Rastafarian Movement*. Chicago: Research Associates School Times Publications and Frontline Distribution International, 1999.

Works Cited

Majority Report of Mission to Africa. Kingston, JA: Government Printer, 1961.

Manley, Michael. *Jamaica: Struggle in the Periphery*. Great Britain: Third World Media, 1982.

———. *The Politics of Change: A Jamaican Testament*. Great Britain: Andre Deutsch, 1974.

———. "Reggae, the Revolutionary Impulse." Introduction. *Reggae International*. Edited by Stephen Davis and Peter Simon. New York: Rogner and Bernhard, 1982. 11–13.

Miles, Robert. *Between Two Cultures?: The Case of Rastafarianism*. Bristol, Eng.: S.S.R.C. Research Unit on Ethnic Relations, 1978.

Morris-Brown, Vivien. *The Jamaica Handbook of Proverbs*. Mandeville, JA: Island Heart, 1993.

Morrish, Ivor. *Obeah, Christ, and Rastaman: Jamaica and Its Religions*. Cambridge, Eng.: J. Clarke, 1982.

Mulvaney, Rebekah M. *Rastafari and Reggae: A Dictionary and Sourcebook*. Westport, Conn.: Greenwood, 1990.

Munroe, Trevor. *The Politics of Constitutional Decolonization: Jamaica, 1944–62*. U of the West Indies, JA: Institute of Social and Economic Research, 1972.

Nagashima, Yoshiko S. *Rastafarian Music in Contemporary Jamaica: A Study of Socioreligious Music of the Rastafarian Movement in Jamaica*. Tokyo, Jap.: Institute for the Study of Languages and Cultures of Asia and Africa, 1984.

National Democratic Movement. 3 Feb. 2000 <http:// www.ndmjamaica.org/ten.html>.

Negril Jamaica: Into the '90's! Chicago: Vacation Network, n.d.

Nettleford, Rex. *Identity, Race and Protest in Jamaica*. New York: William Morrow, 1972.

Owens, Joseph. *Dread: The Rastafarians of Jamaica*. Kingston, JA: Sangster, 1976.

Panton, David. *Jamaica's Michael Manley: The Great Transformation (1972–92)*. Kingston, JA: Kingston Publishers, 1993.

Patterson, Orlando H. *The Children of Sisyphus*. Boston: Houghton Mifflin, 1965.

Payne, Anthony J. *Politics in Jamaica*. London: C. Hurst, 1988.

Permenter, Paris, and John Bigley. *Caribbean for Lovers*. Rocklin: Prima, 1997.

Plummer, John. *Movement of Jah People*. Birmingham, Eng.: Press Gang, 1978.

Porter, Darwin, and Danforth Prince. *Frommer's Jamaica and Barbados*. 3rd ed. New York: Simon and Schuster, 1996.

Post, Ken. *Arise Ye Starvelings: The Jamaican Labour Rebellion of 1938 and Its Aftermath*. Hague: Martinus Nijhoff, 1978.

Quale, Jennifer. "Jamaica." *Berlitz Travellers Guide to the Caribbean*. Edited by Alan Tucker. 6th ed. New York: Berlitz, 1994. 36–67.

Reckord, Verena. "Reggae, Rastafarianism and Cultural Identity." *Reggae, Rasta, Revolution: Jamaican Music from Ska to Dub*. Edited by Chris Potash. New York: Schirmer, 1997. 3–13.

Rimlinger, Gaston V. "The Legitimization of Protest: A Comparative Study in Labor History (1960)." *Protest, Reform, and Revolt: A Reader in Social Movements*. Edited by Joseph R. Gusfield. New York: John Wiley & Sons, 1979. 363–76.

Works Cited

Rodney, Walter. *The Groundings with My Brothers*. 1969. Introduction by Richard Small and Omawale. London: Bogle-L'Ouverture, 1983.

Runstein, Robert E., and David Miles Huber. *Modern Recording Techniques*. 2nd ed. Indianapolis, Ind.: Howard W. Sams, 1986.

Sanders, Rory. "From the Root of King David." *Reggae International*. Edited by Stephen Davis and Peter Simon. New York: Rogner and Bernhard, 1982. 59–68.

Semaj, Leahcim Tufani. "Race and Identity and Children of the African Diaspora: Contributions of Rastafari." *Caribe: West Indians at Home and Abroad*. Edited by Cliff Lashley. New York: Visual Arts Research and Resource Center, 1980. 13–18.

Simons, Herbert W. *Persuasion: Understanding, Practice, and Analysis*. Reading, Mass.: Addison-Wesley, 1976.

Simons, Herbert W., Elizabeth W. Mechling, and Howard N. Schreier. "The Functions of Human Communication in Mobilizing for Action from the Bottom Up: The Rhetoric of Social Movements." *Handbook of Rhetorical and Communication Theory*. Edited by Carroll C. Arnold and John Waite Bowers. Boston: Allyn and Bacon, 1984. 792–867.

Smith, M. G., Roy Augier, and Rex Nettleford. *Report on the Rastafari Movement in Kingston, Jamaica*. U of the West Indies, JA: Department of Extra-Mural Studies, 1978.

Spencer, Jon M. *Protest and Praise: Sacred Music of Black Religion*. Minneapolis, Minn.: Fortress, 1990.

Steffens, Roger M. "Reggae." *All Music Guide: The Best CDs, Albums and Tapes*. Edited by Michael Erlewine and Scott Bultman. San Francisco: Miller Freeman, 1992. 881.

———. "Skatalites." *All Music Guide: The Best CDs, Albums and Tapes*. Edited by Michael Erlewine and Scott Bultman. San Francisco: Miller Freeman, 1992. 894–5.

Stewart, Charles J., Craig Allen Smith, and Robert E. Denton Jr. *Persuasion and Social Movements*. 3rd ed. Prospect Heights: Waveland, 1994.

Stone, Carl. *Class, Race, and Political Behaviour in Urban Jamaica*. U of the West Indies, JA: Institute of Social and Economic Research, 1973.

———. "Power, Policy and Politics in Independent Jamaica." *Jamaica in Independence: Essays on the Early Years*. Edited by Rex Nettleford. Kingston, JA: Heinemann Caribbean, 1989. 19–53.

Thomas, Polly, Adam Vaitilingam, and Adam Vaitilingham. *The Rough Guide to Jamaica*. 2nd ed. 2000. 7 July 2001. <http://travel.roughguides.com/content/12985/30817.htm>.

Ward, Ed, Geoffrey Stokes, and Ken Tucker. *Rock of Ages: The Rolling Stone History of Rock and Roll*. Great Britain: Penguin, 1987.

Waters, Anita M. *Race, Class, and Political Symbols: Rastafari and Reggae in Jamaican Politics*. New Brunswick, N.J.: Transaction, 1985.

White, Garth. "Mento to Ska: The Sound of the City." *Reggae International*. Edited by Stephen Davis and Peter Simon. New York: Rogner and Bernhard, 1982. 37–42.

———. *Traditional Musical Practice in Jamaica and Its Influence on the Birth of Modern Jamaican Popular Music*. Kingston, JA: African-Caribbean Institute of Jamaica, 1982.

Works Cited

———. *The Development of Jamaican Popular Music—Part II*. Kingston, JA: African-Caribbean Institute of Jamaica, 1984.

White, Timothy. *Catch a Fire: The Life of Bob Marley*. Rev. ed. New York: Henry Holt, 1992.

Yawney, Carole D. "Remnants of All Nations: Rastafarian Attitudes to Race and Nationality." *Ethnicity in the Americas*. Edited by Francis Henry. Hague: Mouton, 1976. 231–66.

Journal Articles

Bilby, Kenneth M. "Black Thoughts from the Caribbean: I-deology at Home and Abroad." *New West Indian Guide* 57 (1983): 201–14.

Blacka, Razac (Garth White). "Master Drummer." *Jamaica Journal* 11.1–2 (1977): 16–17.

Broom, Leonard. "The Social Differentiation of Jamaica." *American Sociological Review* 19 (1954): 115–25.

Brodber, Erna. "Black Consciousness and Popular Music in Jamaica in the 1960s and 1970s." *Caribbean Quarterly* 31.2 (1985): 53–66.

Brooks, Cedric. Interview. "Interview with Cedric Brooks." By Shirley M. Burke. *Jamaica Journal* 11.1–2 (1977): 14–17.

Brown, Samuel Elisha. "Treatise on the Rastafarian Movement." *Caribbean Studies* 6.1 (1966): 39–40.

Callam, Neville G. "Invitation to Docility: Defusing the Rastafarian Challenge." *Caribbean Journal of Religious Studies* 3.2 (1980): 28–48.

Campbell, Horace. "Rastafari: Culture of Resistance." *Race and Class* 22.1 (1980): 1–22.

Chevannes, Barry. "Healing the Nation: Rastafari Exorcism of the Ideology of Racism in Jamaica." *Caribbean Quarterly* 36.1–2 (1990): 59–84.

———. "Race and Culture in Jamaica." *World Marxist Review* 31 (1988): 138–44.

Clarke, Colin G. "Dependency and Marginality in Kingston, Jamaica." *Journal of Geography* 82 (1983): 227–35.

Conway, Dennis. "Tourism and Caribbean Development." *Universities Field Staff International* 27 (1983): 1–12.

de Albuquerque, Klaus. "The Future of the Rastafarian Movement." *Caribbean Review* 8.4 (1979): 22–5, 44–6.

de Albuquerque, Klaus, and Jerome L. McElroy. "Caribbean Small-Island Tourism Styles and Sustainable Strategies." *Environmental Management* 16 (1992): 619–32.

Forsythe, Dennis. "West Indian Culture through the Prism of Rastafarianism." *Caribbean Quarterly* 26.4 (1980): 62–81.

Francesconi, Robert A. "James Hunt, the Wilmington 10, and Institutional Legitimacy." *Quarterly Journal of Speech* 68 (1982): 47–59.

Fraser, H. Aubrey. "The Law and Cannabis in the West Indies." *Social and Economic Studies* 5 (1974): 361–85.

Garrison, Len. "The Rastafarians: Journey Out of Exile." *Afras Review* 2.2 (1976): 43–7.

Works Cited

Girvan, Norman. "After Rodney—The Politics of Student Protest in Jamaica." *New World Quarterly* 4.3 (1968): 59–68.

Gonsalves, Ralph. "The Rodney Affair and Its Aftermath." *Caribbean Quarterly* 25.3 (1979): 1–24.

Hall, Douglas. "The Colonial Legacy in Jamaica." *New World Quarterly* 4.3 (1968): 7–23.

Hall, Stuart. "Signification, Representation, Ideology: Althusser and the Post-Structuralist Debates." *Critical Studies in Mass Communication* 2 (1985): 91–114.

Hylton, Patrick. "The Politics of Caribbean Music." *Black Scholar* 7 (1975): 23–9.

I., Ras Dizzy. "The Rastas Speak." *Caribbean Quarterly* 13.4 (1967): 41–2.

Irvine, James R., and Walter G. Kirkpatrick. "The Musical Form in Rhetorical Exchange: Theoretical Considerations." *Quarterly Journal of Speech* 58 (1972): 272–84.

Johnson, Linton K. "The Politics of the Lyrics of Reggae Music." *Black Liberator* 2 (1975): 363–73.

Kaslow, Andrew. "The Roots of Reggae." *Sing Out!* 23.6 (1975): 12–13.

Kaufman, Jay S. "Music and Politics in Jamaica." *Caribbean Review* 15.3 (1987): 9.

King, Andrew A. "The Rhetoric of Power Maintenance: Elites at the Precipice." *Quarterly Journal of Speech* 62 (1976): 127–34.

Knupp, Ralph E. "A Time for Every Purpose under Heaven: Rhetorical Dimensions of Protest Music." *Southern Speech Communication Journal* 46 (1981): 377–89.

Lipsky, Michael. "Protest as a Political Resource." *American Political Science Review* 62 (1968): 1144–58.

Lucas, Stephen E. "Coming to Terms with Movement Studies." *Central States Speech Journal* 31 (1980): 255–66.

Manley, Michael. "A Politician Looks at the Arts." Interview with Basil McFarlane. *Jamaica Journal* 7.1–2 (1973): 42–4.

Nettleford, Rex. "Heritage Tourism: And the Myth of Paradise." *Caribbean Review* 16.3–4 (1990): 8–9.

O'Gorman, Pamela. "On Reggae and Rastafarianism—and a Garvey Prophecy." *Jamaica Journal* 20.3 (1987): 85–7.

Pruitt, Deborah, and Suzanne LaFont. "For Love and Money: Romance Tourism in Jamaica." *Annals of Tourism Research* 22 (1995): 422–40.

Richardson, Mary F. "Out of Many, One People—Aspiration or Reality? An Examination of the Attitudes to the Various Racial and Ethnic Groups within the Jamaican Society." *Social and Economic Studies* 32 (1983): 143–67.

Salaam, Kalamu ya. "Are You Reggae for It Now?" *Black Collegian* 12 (1981): 113–15.

Semaj, Leachim T. "Inside Rasta: The Future of a Religious Movement." *Caribbean Review* 14.1 (1985) 8–11, 37–8.

———. "Rastafari: From Religion to Social Theory." *Caribbean Quarterly* 26.4 (1980): 22–31.

Simons, Herbert W. "Persuasion in Social Conflicts: A Critique of Prevailing Conceptions and a Framework for Future Research." *Speech Monographs* 39 (1972): 227–47.

Works Cited

Simpson, George E. "Political Cultism in West Kingston, Jamaica." *Social and Economic Studies* 4 (1955): 133–49.

White, Garth. "Rudie, Oh Rudie!" *Caribbean Quarterly* 13.3 (1967): 39–44.

Wilson, John. "Social Protest and Social Control." *Social Problems* 24 (1977): 469–81.

Winders, James A. "Reggae, Rastafarians and Revolution: Rock Music in the Third World." *Journal of Popular Culture* 17.1 (1983): 61–73.

Windt, Theodore Otto. "Administrative Rhetoric: An Undemocratic Response to Protest." *Communication Quarterly* 30 (1982): 245–50.

Witmer, Robert. "A History of Kingston's Popular Music Culture: Neo-Colonialism to Nationalism." *Jamaica Journal* 22.1 (1989): 11–18.

Magazine Articles

Bain, Geri. "Jamaica—Romance to the Reggae Beat." *Modern Bride* 1 June-July 1993: 364, 434–40.

Bassford, Andy. "Jamaican Grooves." *How to Play Guitar.* Jan.-Feb. 1996: 43–6.

Cosgrove, Stuart. "Slack-talk and Uptight." *New Stateman and Society* 28 July 1989: 46.

de Albuquerque, Klaus. "In Search of the Big Bamboo: How Caribbean Beach Boys Sell Fun in the Sun." *Utne Reader* Jan.-Feb. 2000: 82–6.

Downs, Joan. "Reggae Power." *Time* 30 Apr. 1973: 79.

Eastham, Kimiko. "Black Culture in Japan." *City Life News Tokyo* Aug. 1993: 2–3.

Egan, Peter. "Racing Jamaica." *Road and Track* June 1997: 269–75.

George, Nelson, and Isaac Fergusson. "Jamming in Jamaica." *Black Enterprise* May 1983: 59–62.

Gorney, Mark. "Jackie Jackson and the Roots of Reggae." *Bass Player* May 1999: 37–41.

Hussey, Dermot. "Bob Marley, The Man of Music for 1975." *Pepperpot* Dec. 1975: 41, 43–5.

Jamaica. Advertisement. *Currents* Winter 1998: 5.

Johnson, Linton K. "The Reggae Rebellion." *New Society* 10 June 1976: 589.

———. "Some Thoughts on Reggae by Linton Kwesi Johnson." *Race Today Review* Dec. 1980/Jan. 1981: 58–61.

Kerridge, Roy. "Marley in Africa." *New Society* 6 Sept. 1985: 343.

Martin, Paul. "High on Jamaica." *National Geographic Traveler* Sept./Oct. 1995: 92–104.

Patterson, Orlando. "The Dance Invasion." *New Society* 15 Sept. 1966: 401–3.

———. "Ras Tafari: The Cult of Outcasts." *New Society* 12 Nov. 1964: 15–17.

Roberts, W. Adolphe. "Portrait of a Jamaican." *Pepperpot* 6 Feb. 1965: 53–5.

Salvo, Barbara, and Patrick Salvo. "Reggae: Jamaican Music in America." *Sepia* Feb. 1974: 36–44.

"Ska—The Up Beat." *Spotlight Newsmagazine* Apr./May 1964: 31–2.

Turner, Dale. "The Skinny on Ska." *Guitar One* Dec. 1997: 147–53.

Vulliamy, Ed. "Roots of Violence." *New Republic* 16 Aug. 1999. Available from *Academic Search Elite* [database on-line]. Accessed 3 February 2000 <http://ehostvgw14.epnet.com/fulltext.asp>.

"Welcome to Paradise, Jamaica-Style." *Economist* 3 Oct. 1998. Available from *Academic Search Elite* [database on-line]. Accessed 3 February 2000 <http://ehostvgw14.epnet.com/fulltext.asp>.

Wexler, Paul L. "Rastafarian Spirit Replacing Violence in Dancehall Lyrics." *Billboard* 19 November 1994. Available from *Academic Search Elite* [database on-line]. Accessed 3 February 2000 <http://ehostvgw14.epnet.com/fulltext.asp>.

Newspaper Articles

"Abeng Sounds a Call to Action." Editorial. *Abeng* 1 Feb. 1969: 1.

Aderemi, Atai. Letter. *Sunday Gleaner* 3 Oct. 1976: 7.

"Agitators Sparked Trouble at Kingston Pen—TAVARES." *Daily Gleaner* 14 Oct. 1963: 1–2.

"At Last." Editorial. *Daily Gleaner* 4 Oct. 1966: 1.

"At Least 20 Dead in Jamaican Violence." *CNN.com.* 10 July 2001. <http://www.cnn.com/2001/WORLD/americas/07/10/jamaica.fighting/index.html>.

Bembridge, Hugh. "Reggae Artists Should Be More Original." Editorial. *Daily Gleaner* 30 Nov. 1975: 8.

Bent, Ras D. "A Poor Man's State in the Rich Men's Kindom [sic]." *Rasta Voice* 6 July 1972: 4.

Blake, Barbara. "Coptics of Star Island: White Rastas." *Sunday Gleaner* 11 May 1980: 1.

"Bob Marley the 'Prophet.'" *Daily Gleaner* 7 Sept. 1976: 4.

Boyne, Ian. "Can Rastafari Survive?" Editorial. *Daily Gleaner* 1 Aug. 1992: 23.

Brown, Howard. Letter. *Daily Gleaner* 21 Oct. 1976: 17.

Brown, Samuel E. Letter. *Daily Gleaner* 10 Sept. 1960: 8.

———. Letter. *Daily Gleaner* 12 May 1966: 10.

"Bulldozers Clear 2 Shanty Towns." *Daily Gleaner* 13 July 1966: 1–2.

Bustamante, Alexander. "This Menace to Our Future." Editorial. *Daily Gleaner* 10 Oct. 1960: 10.

"Cave Mona." Editorial. *Daily Gleaner* 17 Oct. 1968: 8.

"City Getting Back to Normal." *Daily Gleaner* 1 Sept. 1965: 1.

"Curfews, Cordons in Troubled Areas." *Daily Gleaner* 5 Feb. 1976: 1, 19.

"Diary of Events—16th October." *Scope* 18 Oct. 1968: 5–8.

Dizzy, Bongo. "The Voice of the Interpreter: Bongo Dizzy." *Bongo-Man.* Dec. 1968: 14.

Dodds, Suzanne. "Rent a Dread Anyone?" *Daily Gleaner* 20 Jan. 1988: 6.

"Drilled Men Not for Earthly Purposes." *Daily Gleaner* 25 Oct. 1960: 1, 4.

"8 Killed after Attack on Gas Station." *Daily Gleaner* 13 Apr. 1963: 1.

Fearon, Trevor. "Where's the Rip-off?" *Jamaican Daily News* 13 Nov. 1974: 21.

"Forms of Violence." *Abeng* 27 June 1969: 4.

Forsythe, Dennis. "Rastas and the African Lion." *Daily Gleaner* 28 Apr. 1979: 10.

"Ganja Revolution." *Daily Gleaner* 7 Sept. 1976: 3.

Works Cited

Garvey, Marcus Jr. "Black Power: Its Meaning for Jamaica." *Abeng* 1 Mar. 1969: 3.

———. "Marcus Garvey Jnr. Speaks Out!" *Abeng* 21 June 1969: 2.

"Golden Year Likely for Bob Marley and the Wailers." *Daily Gleaner* 25 May 1976: 4.

Grant, Bull. "Brave Woman Denounce Vicious Police Attack on Brethren." *Abeng* 9 Aug. 1969: 2.

Gregory, Colin. "The PM Should Resign." Editorial. *Daily Gleaner* 9 Jan. 1980: 6.

Harris, T. Boots. "Reggae's Growth in the '90s." *Jamaican Record* 4 Aug. 1991: 5C.

Henry, Balford. "This Is 'Dizzy' Johnny Moore." *Sunday Gleaner* 1 Dec. 1985: 4–5.

Henry, Eron. "Rastafari in Eclipse." Editorial. *Daily Gleaner* 2 Dec. 1987: 8.

———. "The Dance-Hall Grip." *Daily Gleaner* 27 Jan. 1988: 9.

Heymans, Peter. "What the Rastaman Sey." *Public Opinion* 12 June 1964: 8.

Historian, Rasta. "African Column." *Bongo-Man* June 1969: 18.

Howell, H. M. Letter. *Daily Gleaner* 5 Sept. 1960: 8.

I., Ras Dizzy. "Revolution or Repatriation?" *Abeng* 13 Sept. 1969: 4.

I, Ras I. "U Blind Yu Cant See [sic]?" Editorial. *Rasta Voice* 14 Jan. 1972: 5.

Jamaica Council for Human Rights. "Protest Raids on Claudius Henry." Editorial. *Daily Gleaner* 15 July 1968: 14.

"Jamaica Officials Fear Loss of Tourism Revenue." *Commercial Appeal* 12 July 2001: A4.

"Jamaican Troops Patrol Capital." *Travel Weekly* 19 July 1999. Available from Academic Search Elite [database on-line]. Accessed 3 February 2000 <http://ehostvgw14.epnet.com/fulltext.asp>.

"Jamaicans Eye Escape from Relentless Crime." *Commercial Appeal* 10 Sept. 2000: A6.

Jerry, Bongo. "Roll on Sweet Don." *Abeng* 17 May 1969: 1.

"JFD Tells of Plot to Overthrow Govt." *Daily Gleaner* 24 June 1980: 1.

Johnson, Barrister Millard. "The Peoples Political Party." Advertisement. *Daily Gleaner* 14 Apr. 1961: 25.

Kassim, Pops. "Police Crime Wave!" *Abeng* 17 May 1969: 3.

Kitchin, Arthur. "Defining Rastafari." Editorial. *Daily Gleaner* 16 June 1983: 8, 13.

———. "A People's Temple in Jamaica?" Editorial. *Daily Gleaner* 19 May 1980: 8, 13.

———. "Rastafari Movement on Trial." Editorial. *Daily Gleaner* 29 Nov. 1982: 8.

———. "Rastas and Politics." Editorial. *Daily Gleaner* 4 June 1979: 6.

"Manley Leads Party to Landslide Win." *Daily Gleaner* 1 Mar. 1972: 1.

"Merry Go Round." Editorial. *Daily Gleaner* 25 Nov. 1975: 4–5.

"Merry Go Round." Editorial. *Daily Gleaner* 14 Aug. 1976: 4, 9.

Parchment, Clinton. "Bearding the Lions of Judah." Editorial. *Daily Gleaner* 11 May 1959: 8.

———. "Rascally Rastafarians." Editorial. *Daily Gleaner* 30 Apr. 1960: 8.

———. "The Rastafarian Psychology." Editorial. *Sunday Gleaner* 4 Dec. 1960: 9.

"PM Lists Five New Govt. Priorities." Daily Gleaner 16 Sept. 1974: 1.

"PM Says It Is Wrong to Cut Rastas' Hair." *Daily Gleaner* 12 Jan. 1976: 15.

"PM, Seaga Join Hands and Dance." *Daily Gleaner* 24 Apr. 1978: 1, 11.

"Police Destroy Rasta Houses." *Abeng* 8 Mar. 1969: 1.

Rasta Voice Editorial Board. No title. Editorial. *Rasta Voice* 14 Jan. 1972: 4.

Works Cited

"A Rasta Youth Speaks." *Daily Gleaner* 27 Sept. 1976: 8.

"Rastafarians Seek Action from PM." *Daily Gleaner* 16 June 1976: 2.

"Rastas Meet with PM." *Daily Gleaner* 19 Mar. 1976: 9.

Ritch, Dawn. "Middle-Class Prejudice?" Editorial. *Daily Gleaner* 15 Mar. 1979: 6.

———. "Something Worth Talking About." Editorial. *Daily Gleaner* 19 Jan. 1978: 6.

Rodney, Walter. "The Rise of Black Power in the West Indies." *Abeng* 8 Mar. 1969: 3.

"Rose Hall." Editorial. *Daily Gleaner* 13 Apr. 1963: 10.

Rosenberg, Matthew J. "Hard Times, Crime Drive Exodus of Jamaican Middle Class." *Commercial Appeal* 8 Dec. 1999: B4.

———. "Bob Marley's Legacy Grows as Jamaicans Celebrate 55th Anniversary of His Birth." *Post Register* 6 Feb. 2000: A2.

"Seaga Thanks Marley." *Daily Gleaner* 27 Apr. 1978: 2.

"Seven Die in Jamaican Neighborhood Shooting." *Post Register* 21 Aug. 2001: A10.

Shea, Barbara. "Is Tourism Too Much of a Good Thing? Vacation Spots Must Strive to Protect, Preserve Environments and Cultures." *Commercial Appeal.* 2 May 1999. 29 Jan. 2000 <http://www.gomemphis.com>.

"Shearer Says Govt. Will Not Withdraw Order; Statement Today in House." *Daily Gleaner* 17 Oct. 1968: 1, 7.

Showman. "'Reggae' on Broadway." *Daily Gleaner* 25 Mar. 1980: 4.

"State of Emergency in West Kingston." *Daily Gleaner* 4 Oct. 1966: 1.

"Stokely and the Black Panthers." *Abeng* 12 July 1969: 1.

Strong, Matthew. "Get It Right." Editorial. *Daily Gleaner* 10 Mar. 1961: 12.

Strong, William. "You Can Quote Me." Editorial. Daily Gleaner 8 Oct. 1963: 10.

———. "You Can Quote Me." Editorial. Daily Gleaner 10 Oct. 1963: 8.

"Students 'Consider Themselves above the Law.'" *Daily Gleaner* 2 Nov. 1968: 14.

Tafari, Jabulani I. "Jimmy Cliff 'Liberates' Soweto." *Daily Gleaner* 2 Sept. 1980: 4.

"Text of Shearer's Speech at JLP Parley." *Daily Gleaner* 25 Nov. 1968: 10, 22.

Trumann, Thomas. "The Sting of Joshua's Rod." Editorial. *Daily Gleaner* 11 Jan. 1980: 6.

Tucker, Gil. "Rastas Must Unite." Editorial. *Rasta Voice* 9 Aug. 1974: 2.

Walters, Basil. "Is the RastafarI Culture on the Decline?" Editorial. *Sunday Gleaner* 9 Aug. 1992: 12A.

"Watch Word Should Be Love." *Star* 25 May 1961: 6–7.

"Weapons Seized in Raid on Church Headquarters." *Daily Gleaner* 7 Apr. 1960: 1, 14.

Webster, Paul C. "Rise in Violence in Jamaica Prompts Anti-Crime Initiative." *New York Amsterdam News* 9 Sept. 1999. Available from *Academic Search Elite* [database on-line]. Accessed 3 February 2000 <http://ehostvgw14.epnet.com/fulltext.asp>.

"The World Discovers Reggae." *Sunday Gleaner* 2 Dec. 1975: 4.

Wright, Tomas. "Candidly Yours." Editorial. *Daily Gleaner* 27 Nov. 1968: 14.

Works Cited

Government Documents

Jamaica. Census Research Programme. *Life Tables for British Caribbean Countries, 1959–61*. Kingston, JA: U of the West Indies, 1966.

Jamaica. Jamaica Town Planning Department Report 1961/62. *Town Planning Department Report for Financial Year April 1st 1961–31st March 1962*. Kingston, JA: Government Printer.

Jamaica. National Planning Agency. *Economic Survey of Jamaica, 1972*. Kingston, JA: Government Printer.

Jamaica. National Planning Agency. *Economic and Social Survey Jamaica, 1975*. Kingston, JA: Government Printer.

Jamaica. National Planning Agency. *Economic and Social Survey Jamaica, 1977*. Kingston, JA: Government Printer.

Convention Paper

Gibson, Dirk. "I and I Downpressor Man: Reggae as an Instrument of Social Change." Intercultural/International Communication Conference. Florida. Jan. 1990.

Music, Television and Film

Abyssinians. *Satta Massagana*. Heartbeat, 1993.

Barrow, Steve. Liner notes. *Tougher Than Tough: The Story of Jamaican Music*. Island, 1993.

Bob Marley: Rebel Music. American Masters Special. PBS. 14 Feb. 2001.

The Bob Marley Story: Caribbean Nights. Dir. T. Wall and Anthony Finch. Island, 1985.

Culture. *Two Sevens Clash*. Shanachie, 1978/1988.

Duke Reid's Treasure Chest. Heartbeat, 1992.

The Harder They Come. LP. Island, 1972.

History of Trojan Records, 1968–1971. Trojan, 1995.

Jingles, Julian. Liner notes. *Ska Bonanza: The Studio One Ska Years*. Heartbeat, 1991.

The "King" Kong Compilation: The Historic Reggae Recordings, 1968–1970. Island, 1981.

Life and Debt. PBS. 21 Aug. 2001.

Marley, Bob, and the Wailers. *The Bob Marley and the Wailers Collection, Vol. 3*. Distributions Madacy, n.d.

———. *Exodus*. LP. Island, 1977.

———. *Kaya*. LP. Island, 1978.

———. *Natty Dread*. Audiocassette. Island, 1975.

———. *One Love at Studio One*. Heartbeat, 1991.

———. *Rastaman Vibration*. LP. Island, 1976.

———. *Survival*. Audiocassette. Island, 1979.

———. *Talkin' Blues*. Audiocassette. Tuff Gong, 1991.

————. *Uprising*. Tuff Gong, 1980.

Masters of Reggae. Audiocassette. Distributions Madacy, n.d.

Maytals, Toots. *Funky Kingston*. Audiocassette. Island, 1973.

Ska Bonanza: The Studio One Ska Years. Heartbeat, 1991.

Spear, Burning. *100th Anniversary*. Island, 1990.

Stepping Razor—Red X: The Peter Tosh Story. Dir. Nicholas Campbell. Northern Arts Entertainment, 1992.

Tosh, Peter. *Equal Rights*. CBS, 1977.

————. *Legalize It*. CBS, 1976.

————. *Mama Africa*. CBS, 1983.

————. *The Toughest*. Capitol, 1988.

Tougher Than Tough: The Story of Jamaican Music. Island, 1993.

Uhuru, Black. *Red*. Island, 1981.

————. *Sinsemilla*. Island, 1980.

Wailer, Bunny. *Blackheart Man*. Island, 1976.

Wailers. *Burnin'*. LP. Island, 1973.

————. *Catch a Fire*. LP. Island, 1973.

Interviews

Chevannes, Barry. Personal Interview. 6 July 1994.

Cooper, Carolyn. Personal Interview. 5 July 1994.

Hussey, Dermot. Personal Interview. 18 July 1994.

Nettleford, Rex. Personal Interview. 23 July 1994.

INDEX

"Birth Control," 64
"Black and White," 58
Black Arks, The, "Come Along," 59
Black Power Movement (Jamaica), 46,
    50–52, 81, 83, 89; influence of
    America's Black Power Movement
    on, 48; Rastafarian Movement's
    critical reaction to, 52, 81, 83
"Black Starliner Must Come," 96
Black Uhuru, 97
"Blackhead Chinee Man," 17
Blackheart Man (album), 96
Blackwell, Chris, 54, 95, 96, 143;
    marketing of reggae, 98, 99. *See also*
    Island Records
"Blood & Fire," 55, 57, 58, 64
Bob and Marcia, "Young Gifted &
    Black," 60, 62
Bob Marley and the Wailers: "Africa
    Unite," 97; "Ambush in the Night,"
    97; *Bob Marley and the Wailers
    Collection, Vol. 3, The* (album),
    57–59, 73, 74; "Could You Be
    Loved," 99; *Exodus* (album), 99, 128,
    137; "Exodus" (song), 99, 137; Natty
    Dread (album), xiii, 99; "No Woman
    No Cry," xiii; "One Love" (song),
    40, 128; *One Love at Studio One*
    (album) 17–18, 37–41, 44; "Punky
    Reggae Party," 101; *Rastaman
    Vibration* (album), xiii, 97; "Rat
    Race," xiii; "Redemption Song," 99;
    "So Much Trouble in the World,"
    97; *Survival* (album), 97, 101;
    "Talkin' Blues" (song), 99; *Uprising*
    (album), 99; "War," 97; "Zimbabwe,"
    97, 101. *See also* Marley, Bob;
    Wailers, The
Bongo-Man (newspaper), 50–52
Boothe, Ken: "Freedom Street," 58, 60;
    "The Train Is Coming," 39, 41, 42
Brooks, Baba, "Gun Fever," 37
Brooks, Cedric, 102

Brown, Samuel, 32, 33, 84
Burnin' (album), xiii, 98
Burning Spear, xi; *Garvey's Ghost*
    (album), 96; *Marcus Garvey*
    (album), 96; *100th Anniversary*
    (album), 96; "Slavery Days," 96
Bustamante, Alexander, 6, 7, 75
Bustamante Industrial Trade Union
    (BITU), 6
Buster, Prince, 20; "Barrister Pardon,"
    38, 39; "Blackhead Chinee Man,"
    17; "Judge Dread," 38, 39; "Too
    Hot," 37, 38
Byles, Junior, "Beat Down Babylon,"
    56, 58
Byron Lee and the Dragonaires, 73

Carmichael, Stokely, 27, 48
Carrington, Vernon, 53
"Carry Go Bring Come," xiii, 19, 20,
    22, 23
Catch a Fire (album), xiii, 55, 96, 99
"Catch a Fire" (song), 96
censorship, xiii, xiv, 4
Central Intelligence Agency (CIA),
    93, 147 n
Centralizing Committee of the
    Rastafarian Selassie I Divine
    Theocratic Government, 110, 111
Charmers, The, 14
Checkmates, The, "Turn Me On," 16, 17
"Cherry Oh Baby," 62, 64
Clapton, Eric, 101; "I Shot the
    Sheriff," 101
Clash, The, 101
Cleaver, Eldridge, 27, 48
Cliff, Jimmy, 19, 22, 101; "Miss
    Jamaica," 22; "Wonderful World,
    Beautiful People," 54
coercive persuasion, 67, 78. *See also*
    social movements
colonialism, xi, 5–9, 68, 69, 111, 139,
    140. *See also* neo-colonialism

"One Love," 40
One Love at Studio One (album), 17,
  18, 37–40, 44
One Love Peace Concert, xii, 113, 117
Operation Bootstrap, 8
Operation Buccaneer, 117
Operation Grow, 100
Operation Intrepid, 132
Operational Shantytown, 29
Orange Street Massacre, 93
"Over the River," 18, 23

patois, xx, 46, 54
Patterson, P. J., 132, 133
People's National Party (PNP), xii,
  132, 137, 146 n, 147 n; campaign
  songs banned by JLP, 73; campaign
  songs of, 108; development of, 6–8;
  gang members as political
  supporters, 30, 113; impact of
  international reggae on, 104; neo-
  colonialism, 69; response to
  Rastafarians' request for repatriation,
  116; weekly musical political
  bandwagon, 108
People's Political Party (PPP), 6
Perry, Lee "Scratch," 54; as a producer,
  59; "Sugar Bag," 16
Pinnacle Community, xviii-xx
Platters, The, 14
police. *See* Rastafarian Movement
political parties. *See* Jamaica Labour
  Party (JLP); National Democratic
  Movement (NDM); People's
  National Party (PNP); People's
  Political Party (PPP)
political violence, 93–95, 132, 133
"Power for the People," 108
"Pressure Drop," 56
"Promises, Promises," 116
protest lyrics. *See* reggae, early; reggae,
  international

protest music theory, 142–44. *See also*
  Rastafarian Movement; reggae, early;
  reggae, international
pseudo Rastafarians. *See* Rastafarian
  Movement
Public Opinion (newspaper), 13
punk movement. *See* Rastafarian
  Movement; reggae, international
"Punky Reggae Party," 101

"Queen Majesty," 41–43

Radio Jamaica Rediffusion Limited
  (RJR), 72, 118
radio stations (Jamaica), banning and
  marginalizing reggae songs, xiii, xiv,
  57, 65, 72–74, 118–19. *See also*
  Jamaica Broadcasting Corporation
  (JBC); Radio Jamaica Rediffusion
  Limited (RJR)
ragga music, 120, 133
Ranks, Cutty, 89
Ranks, Shabba, 133
Ras Dizzy I. *See* I., Ras Dizzy
Ras Tafari Makonnen. *See* Haile
  Selassie I
"Rasta Historian," 52
Rasta Voice (newspaper): advocating of
  repatriation, 52, 53; critique of
  Walter Rodney, 81; establishment of,
  46, 52, 83; political agenda, 53;
  reaction to UWI students and
  faculty activities, 52
Rastafarian Movement: arrests/police
  intimidation of members, xvi, xvii,
  xix-xxi, 11–13, 25, 29, 35, 51, 67,
  78–81, 111; change in repatriation
  plan (Liberation Before
  Repatriation), 28, 32, 34, 52, 66, 67;
  colors, 11, 127, 128; co-optation of,
  106–15, 121, 122, 135, 136, 144;
  critical reaction to Black Power